Mark
One Ordinary Life—
Extraordinary *Grace*

outskirts
press

One Ordinary Life—Extraordinary Grace
All Rights Reserved.
Copyright © 2023 Mark J. Schreiber
v7.0

The opinions expressed in this manuscript are solely the opinions of the author and do not represent the opinions or thoughts of the publisher. The author has represented and warranted full ownership and/or legal right to publish all the materials in this book.

This book may not be reproduced, transmitted, or stored in whole or in part by any means, including graphic, electronic, or mechanical without the express written consent of the publisher except in the case of brief quotations embodied in critical articles and reviews.

Outskirts Press, Inc.
http://www.outskirtspress.com

ISBN: 978-1-9772-6254-7

Cover Photo © 2023 istock. All rights reserved - used with permission.

From the book, *Why We Fight: Moral Clarity and the War on Terrorism*, updated edition, by William J. Bennett. Copyright © 2002 William J. Bennett. Used by permission of Regnery Publishing.

Concordia Commentary: Luke 9:51-24:53 © 1997 Concordia Publishing House. Used with permission.

Outskirts Press and the "OP" logo are trademarks belonging to Outskirts Press, Inc.

PRINTED IN THE UNITED STATES OF AMERICA

Table of Contents

Introduction: The Eye of the Needle i
Preface vii
One Ordinary Life: Extraordinary Grace The Day of Baptism .. xiii

PART ONE: Of Grace, Unawares
    Love Launched! 2
    Why I Became a Monk 4
    First Kiss 6
    The Bike Fight 8
    The Take Down 13
    Laughter . . . Still the Best Medicine 16
    Old Days 20
    Footprints of Sorrow 33
    The Runaway 36
    Barracuda Bust 41
    Hitchin' a Ride 44
    Lights Out 46

PART TWO: Grace Manifested
    Searching for Truth 50
    Forsake All! 54
    Return to Lincoln Land 56
    Ambition to Excel 58
    Holy Toledo! 59
    A Lot of Learning is a Good Thing! 62
    Bethel Lutheran Church Glenshaw, Pennsylvania 64
    MAG 29 Active Duty 70
    Helo Down Over I-95 78

Unbridled Ambition 81
Recalled! 86
Life aboard a Super Carrier 90
Danger Zone 93
Whiffle Bat and Angels 96
Short Skirts, Perfume and High Heels 99
Dependents Day Cruise 101
Pass Over 105
Guardian Lutheran Church, Jacksonville, Florida 111
German to the Rescue 118
Public High School Teacher—Full Time 123
Chewed Out 126
One Loose Screw Secured 129
8th Marine Corps Recruiting District 130
Evangelism—Marine Corps Style 134
Divine Linkage 136
The New World of Endorsing Agent 139
Postscriptum 146

Epilogue 150
Appendix 1 154
Appendix 2 155
Appendix 3 158
Appendix 4 162
Appendix 5 163

One Ordinary Life is a wonderful book and a great read. Chaplain Schreiber carries you back into his life making you feel like you are right there with him as he reminisces on how God has used "ordinary" events in the author's "ordinary life" to bring extraordinary grace to serve Him and His people wherever we are called to serve. Our vocations "callings" are not really "ordinary" in God's plan. He will use us to bring the Gospel to those whom God puts into our lives, no matter how "ordinary" we think we are. You need to read *One Ordinary Life—Extraordinary Grace*, share it with others, and bask in the knowledge that God has used you in His kingdom.

Chaplain Craig G. Muehler,
CAPT, CHC, USN (Ret.)

Many of us know (Captain, US Navy, Ret.) Chaplain Mark Schreiber as the author of *Nailed!: Moral Injury: A Response from the Cross of Christ for the Combat Veteran*. Some of us know him as a brother pastor who has, with *Nailed!*, blessed us with an invaluable Christ-centered resource for ministering to our combat veterans who suffer the nearly invisible moral injuries that afflict countless modern warriors. Others of you know him as your chaplain on the aircraft carrier USS Theodore Roosevelt CVN-71.

How does an ordinary little boy become an official voice of God almighty, a voice of the world's one and only Savior to thousands of souls onboard a floating, mobile combat airfield – a fortress of a platform which is a means by which our country delivers power and protection to the uttermost parts of the earth?

The briefest answer is: It is all by God's grace. Captain Scheiber's wonderfully expanded response is an extraordinarily personal example of God's grace at work on the person-to-person level: It is all by God's grace which He brings to us via the means of grace, namely, God's Word and the sacrament of Baptism. It is all by God's grace that He calls ordinary men such as Chaplain Mark Schreiber, to deliver the "force multiplier" of God's Word and sacraments to men and women in the profession of arms.

The life story of this book is the story of God's extraordinary work in and through an ordinary man who answered the divine call to strengthen and to counsel, to reprove and to forgive those who wear the uniform – those who suffer injuries, visible and invisible, in the course of their service to God, family, and country. It is the life story of one man who wears the armor of God and His Word (Ephesians 6) and who is at the same time a healer of wounded and suffering souls. In the ministry, we call such a man "Seelsorger," German for "healer of Souls." In the military we call such a man "chaplain."

You have in your hands not only an autobiography that will inspire another generation of chaplains. You are also holding a book that will minister to you as you yourself suffer injuries, visible and invisible to others. This is because you are holding a book by a quietly extraordinary man, made what he is by God's grace. This is a book that will convince you of the truth that God's grace is active in your ordinary life as well.

Rev. Gregory P Schulz,
DMin, PhD; Lt Col USAF/
CAP (ret.); author of
The Problem of Suffering

Introduction:
The Eye of the Needle

Your angle of approach to the flight deck, called your glide slope, is absolutely critical for a safe carrier landing at sea. Too steep and you will hit the deck with such terrific force that your plane may break apart. Too shallow and you will hit the rounded approach ramp at the stern of the ship and spew broken plane parts, jet fuel, and weapons across the flight deck. Either approach would be catastrophic for the crew and for many hands on the flight deck. Your aim is to penetrate the eye of the needle.

The "meatball" is the Navy's answer to threading the eye of the needle for a perfect carrier landing. The "meatball" or Light Landing Device (LLD) is a stationary optical visual in the midst of a moving and rolling flight deck at sea. Positioned on the port side of the flight deck, the pilot "calls the ball" when it becomes visible within a mile of the flight deck. The colored lenses of the "meatball" guide the pilot's eyes down an optical glide slope signaling him whether he is too high, too low and the horizontal relationship of his wings to the flight deck. Dangling out the rear of his plane, twenty or more feet below the pilot, protrudes the tailhook like an eagle's claw waiting to catch an arresting cable drawn taut across the flight deck.

The LSO (Landing Signal Officer) is the pilot's eyes on the flight deck. Positioned at the stern of the ship, port side, surrounded by canvass safety nets and fore of the meatball, he is the final authority on approach. In his hand is the "pickle switch" which lights up the meatball in a cluster of red lights signaling a wave-off to the pilot and to begin another approach.

If the approaching jet is an F-14 Tomcat, the pilot eases the jet down the glide slope, maneuvering 61,000 pounds of metal at an approach speed of approximately 130+ knots. He lines up his Tomcat with the angled deck of the carrier to touch down on a postage-stamp runway of about 600 feet. As soon as the wheels hit the flight deck the pilot pushes the throttles forward to full power. If his tailhook has successfully seized a cable, he brings the engines back to idle, and the deck hands guide the plane to its parking place on the flight deck. If his tailhook has missed all four cables, he "bolters." With engines at full throttle, the fighter jet screams down the flight deck, clears the runway and banks to port circling for another approach.

From the standpoint of the ship's crew, as well as that of the pilots, the recovery of aircraft is the climax of carrier operations; it is the eye of the needle through which they must pass. By the general consent of those involved and those who only observe, it is the most difficult trick in aviation.[1]

USS Theodore Roosevelt CVN-71, Cruisebook, 1987.

---

1 Peter Garrison. *Carrier Aviation.* (San Rafael, California: Presidio Press, 1980), 41. See the author's vivid detailed description of carrier landing operations as described in chapter three of *Carrier Aviation* entitled, "The Dance on the Deck."

No, I am not a Navy fighter pilot even though it was once a short-lived dream of mine. I am only an observer, a Navy chaplain, a plank owner who served aboard USS Theodore Roosevelt CVN-71 from 1986-1988 and observed hundreds of jet launches and recoveries from the island above her flight deck.

To land a jet aircraft safely on the rolling, moving flight deck of a super carrier at sea within the short space of 600 feet is to thread the eye of the needle every time. Ten thousand times ten thousand this dangerous drama has been repeated in the history of American carrier aviation. No nation on earth can boast the same accomplishment. It is simply extraordinary. This drama at sea viewed through the right lens, can have incredible spiritual significance for your life.

Allow me the power of analogy utilizing the lens of carrier operations. Imagine now that the flight deck represents your safe haven in life, the place you return to again and again for meaning and stability. The flight deck is the source and script of God's mission for your life. God is the Air Boss who catapults and launches every new mission. God's script for your life is better than your self-imagined, self-imposed script. God's loving script for you is a miraculous script written by His own hand, an extraordinary script beyond your wildest dreams and imaginations. Without God's script engaging your life, the bolters and the wave-offs in your life's vocation will be frequent and painful. And the traps by the arresting cables of God's grace on the safe haven of His celestial flight deck will be few.

What do you really want out of life? Do you want to engage God's extraordinary script and receive His marvelous blessings all the days of your life or do you just want to slug it out through life's upheavals, hoping you will hit the flight deck safely once in a while in the midst of the storm? Take the chance without God's script and you will bolter again and again, run low on fuel with the deadly imminent danger of ditching your plane into the turbulent angry sea.

For me to say to you, "The choice is yours," would be far too simple and simplistic. God's answer is much more complex, often counter-intuitive against all the powers of human reasoning. God's answer begins the day you were baptized into Christ Jesus.

Consider this. If landing a fighter jet on the rolling flight deck of a carrier at sea can be compared to the difficulty of threading the eye of a needle, then Christ Jesus has something very important to say to you about your entrance into the kingdom of God. He said that it would be easier for a camel to pass through the eye of a needle than for a rich man to enter the kingdom of God.[2]

Easier, you say? Can you imagine trying to squeeze a camel, fully loaded or not, through the eye of a needle? The comparison is incredulous, beyond belief, in fact, it is impossible. And that's the point.[3] No one will enter the kingdom of God, despite your status rich or poor, unless God miraculously intervenes doing the impossible task of threading your soul through the eye of the needle.

How can this be true? If human intelligence and the vaunted great American know-how[4] can figure out how to do the near impossible task of landing a jet within 600 feet of flight deck, how much more do you think that God, the supreme omniscient architect of the universe can save your soul by threading the eye of the needle pulling you into His kingdom through the wonderful script that He has already written for your ordinary life?

How God threads the eye of the needle and saves our souls is exactly what this little book is all about. Or to put it in Navy carrier-speak; how God will use His better script for the unfolding events of your life

---

2 Matthew 19:24, Mark 10:25, Luke 18:25.
3 Arthur A. Just Jr. *Concordia Commentary Luke 9:51-24:53*. (St. Louis, Missouri: Concordia Publishing House, 1997). p. 699. Dr. Just writes, "Jesus is telling the rich man and all hearers of the Word that the kingdom is inaccessible for human beings without the miraculous intervention of God."
4 Garrison, *Carrier Aviation*, 28. Garrison cites a carrier officer stating the military's assessment of its own military prowess: "We could give the Russians this whole ship and every airplane on it, and it would be fifteen years before they could figure out how to use it." Those words were penned 43 years ago. Not much has changed in the armed forces capacity of the Russians to build, launch and maintain a single Russian aircraft carrier.

to trap you by your tailhook via the cable of God's arresting grace upon His celestial flight deck. God alone threads the needle. He calls all the shots as you approach the stern of His ship. He alone traps you safely and does the impossible. To God be all the glory.

Preface

There were only three chaplains in the CRMD[5] for most of my tour of duty aboard USS Theodore Roosevelt CVN-71. Rotating through three chaplains for "prayer duty" meant that every third night at sea, I would have the *Conn*[6] on the bridge and be given the 1MC[7] for the singular duty of offering an evening prayer heavenward on behalf of the ship and her crew. Sixty seconds and no more was my personal time limit but it is amazing what can be said in sixty seconds if your prayer is well thought out and written down in advance. Learning to speak the crew's language and connect with their world pays great dividends and projects the chaplain as a spiritual "force multiplier" in the mind of the crew and its officers. Here is one prayer offered heavenward during a two month deployment early in 1987, delivered precisely at 2200 hours while TR was deployed at sea:

Heavenly Father,

TOPGUN professionalism. Efficiency and competence.
20 plus tons of angry steel hurtling down the bow cat.
Nimble fingers prancing lightly over the controls:

CAT—READY . . . BRIDLE TENSION—READY.
MILITARY POWER—READY . . . FINAL SALUTE—READY.

---

5   CRMD is the Navy acronym for the Command Religious Ministries Department.
6   *Conn* is Navy slang for "Control" that is, to have control of the ship or as in metonymy, the ship's bridge, the place where total control of the ship happens.
7   1MC: One Main Circuit, (see footnote 72).

All the players are ready, frozen motionless in time. The CAT is fired. Bird's away. America's defense is on the move.

Dear Lord, the drama of launch and recovery is repeated thousands of times in the life of an aircraft carrier. Get us ready, O Lord, for the launch of faith, daring in design, bold in execution, recklessly trusting your Word—your promise—so that even against all the odds in life and in the blackest night, you will do for us just as you have promised.

I AM THE LORD, THY GOD,
STAND BESIDE ME AND SEE MY SALVATION.

We stand ready on the CAT of life, O Lord.

Launch our faith.

We are ready now.

Amen.

*F-14 Tomcats launched from the flight deck of
USS Theodore Roosevelt CVN-71 at sea, Cruisebook, 1987.*

Dedication

To all,
who are being threaded
and to all who will be threaded
through the eye of the needle into the Kingdom of God
to land safely on the flight deck
of His celestial grace.

Epigraph

It is easier for a camel to go through the eye of a needle
than for a rich man to enter the kingdom of God.
Matthew 19:24

We are His workmanship, created in Christ Jesus for good works,
which God prepared (scripted) beforehand
that we should walk in them.
Ephesians 2:10

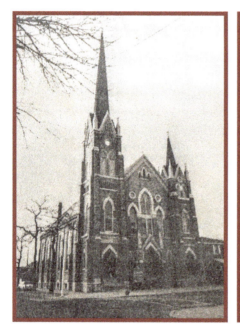
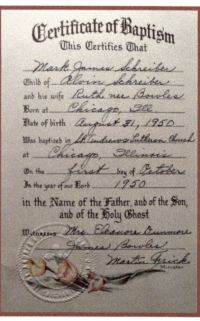

One Ordinary Life: Extraordinary Grace
The Day of Baptism

October 1st, 1950, Chicago, Illinois. *On a beautiful Fall Sunday morning, one month after birth, my godly parents brought their infant son to the waters of baptism at St. Andrew Lutheran Church. Then and there at that moment in time, the extraordinary grace of God in Christ Jesus entered my heart, my mind and my soul. The script of my life began.*

October 1st, 1954, Toledo, Ohio. *Four years later, the love of my earthly life, Connie Ann Cramer, was born. I would not meet Connie until twenty one years later, 1975, while rushing through the church doors at Good Shepherd Lutheran Church in Toledo on a Sunday morning in August as the church's new vicar. I was always in a hurry and almost bowled her over. A couple of months later on our first date and our first kiss, her lips won first prize in my heart. Nothing has changed since. God's grace is extraordinary for every ordinary life. For every event His timing is perfect. His script is a good script. Here begins the compelling evidence of my life. The tapestry of your life is no less compelling. Seek His evidence! Your discovery will be grand!*

Baptism is the dawn of a new reality filled with the presence of God and His mighty angels. Baptism gives you a new identity, a new posture toward life, a new face on life. Baptism is the ever flowing cataract of God's overflowing love in Christ which washes and scrubs you clean of every sin every moment of every day. Baptism launches you from the celestial flight deck of God's grace into this troubled world. Yes, Baptism does all these things through Christ Jesus.

Launch our faith, dear Lord!

My loving parents, Alvin and Ruth, who brought Neil (on the right) and me to the waters of Baptism. Neil would join the Marines in 1964 and serve two tours of combat in Vietnam.

PART ONE:
Of Grace, Unawares

Love Launched!

"Many waters cannot quench love."
Song of Songs 8:7

Let me paint the picture.

She was the most beautiful woman my young eyes had ever seen. There was grace in every step she took. Even the slow-moving, low-hanging, charcoal-grey streaked clouds of Chicago could not darken her smile because she always put a dazzling new face on the day below. She was sunshine. She was angelic. She was a delight to look upon. I was in love and quite sure that she felt the same way about me. The smell of her perfume, the sweetness of her voice, the way she put her arms around me and hugged me close all forecasted one sure and certain event—someday we would be married and live happily ever after! Just knowing that I would see her daily at school put eager anticipation into every step. She was the love of my life, no other love could come between us. It was simply unthinkable. Yes, young we both were but love is patient, love is timeless, love conquers all. Destiny awaited us. The day of wedded bliss and happiness was firmly fixed on the calendar of my mind when our lives would be threaded together. I think you get the picture.

Miss Kaiser, my beloved Kindergarten infatuation.

Now you can imagine how devastated I was when I heard the rumor that the love of my life was planning to marry another and she hadn't even consulted me. Had she not promised to marry me? Had she not said that she would wait the necessary years before we could both proceed to God's altar? Well, at least she implied it!

Was the rumor true? Yes, it was and I was crushed. My kindergarten teacher, Miss Kaiser, was planning to marry another man by the name of Mr. Boschline. Sure, he was much older than I and already had a steady income but what is that compared to the passions of true love? I was five years old and Miss Kaiser twenty-two.

Who was this beautiful woman who graced the halls of St. Andrew Lutheran School, 37th Honore, on the southside of Chicago? Miss Kaiser by name, the new Kindergarten teacher and I her prize pupil, the apple of her eye, or at least I thought so. The year? 1955. That September promised to be a very good year but by next Spring the new grapes of love had turned sour.

Well, whenever a young heart is broken there is only one recourse, ridicule! Ridicule fights back! Ridicule stabs the soul. Ridicule creates pain and pity but ridicule might bring success! All my classmates could see my broken heart and joined in the sarcastic fun. Boschline rhymed with "clothesline" so now my new suitor's name who had vanquished me would be, "Mr. Clothesline." Miss Kaiser had dumped me and would marry Mr. Clothesline. I had been hung out to dry and left blowing in the wind. Or to use a football analogy, I had been taken out of the play, devastated by a clothesline tackle above the waist that broke my heart.

Now you may think that such puppy love is cute silly nonsense and my depiction of it pure hyperbole (and it is!) but puppy love is still real to the puppy. I'm sure your heart can relate to my feelings at the ripe old age of five when all my marital plans had been tossed into the dumpster, my future completely dark and uncertain and the path ahead bleak and forlorn. All this gushing forth from the heart of a five year old boy! How many years of therapy would it take to heal my heart?! Only God knows. Nevertheless, God, the Author of all love, would prevail. His plan far exceeds the first rumblings of passion in our hearts. Although for me, the divine future did not include the lovely Miss Kaiser it most certainly included something even more lovely; namely, the extraordinary grace of God flowing through one simple ordinary life, day by day. Better footprints lie ahead. The lovesick puppy eventually does grow up.

I had been launched into love from the celestial flight deck of God's grace. Many would be the bolters across His flight deck of love. Nevertheless, the script of His divine love could not be broken nor fail. God penetrated the eye of the needle that led me ultimately to the day I would meet Connie.

I have good news for your love life. The many waters of fickle love is surpassed by God's unquenchable love for you. His plan is good. His script is extraordinary. Threading the eye of the needle of love is easy for God.

Why I Became a Monk

"It is better to marry than to burn with passion (!)"
1 Cor. 7:9

Needless to say, my parents could not find a therapist who would take their hard earned cash and guarantee a cure for the broken heart of a five year old boy. So it seemed that my short life on earth was now irretrievably destined to be traumatized by lovesickness and all its attendant morose consequences. *Ahhh,* what would become of me?

WHY I BECAME A MONK

Who would embrace me? Comfort me? Love me? Feed me? Dry my tears and cuddle me? Of course, a five year old boy doesn't see these questions as replete with overweening dangerous narcissism (even if he could spell the word), rather they are just the relentless cries of his young heart lost in a world of melancholy and lovesick blues. Then the day arrived when Grandma asked a question for this young life that demanded an immediate answer.

"So, tell me Mark, what are you going to be when you grow up?"

What a momentous moment in the history of the English speaking world! What breathtaking thoughts seeking verbal formation cascaded through the smooth, supple contours of my young brain! What astounding answer would now dribble forth from the tip of my tongue?

Grandma waited. Grandma smiled. Grandma got my answer.

"I'm going to be a pastor, Grandma!" That was it. The word was out. I didn't understand where the word had come from but there it was, out in the open. A pastor, no other answer, no other vocation for my life. So it has been, all my life to this day. No doubt about it.

It was the perfect solution for broken hearts. Pastors, that is, Lutheran pastors, don't have to get married. They are free to be celibate. I could be a monk by choice! Away with romance, away with melancholy, away with the blues! No longer would my heartstrings be tied to fickle women. Now I could immerse myself in my books, drown myself in ethereal thoughts of sublime wordplay, nuancing deeper and deeper thoughts until

Grandpa and Grandma Schreiber

someday, standing in the pulpit, I could pontificate to others about the blissful lofty grandiose life of celibacy and the extreme dangers of wasting time chasing fickle romance. Grandma had saved my soul and set the course of my life on a new uncharted direction.

God's first major footprint for my love life had been revealed. Monkhood! No doubt about it. Glorified celibacy! But romance and passion, as you know, die a slow, slow death. And as for me, it was not dead yet, in fact it would never die, but here's the difference. God would rethread my love and passions through the eye of the needle demonstrating His best love for me making the impossible, possible. I would learn that His script of love was far better than any I could have written for myself. But first a few more bolters off the flight deck of love.

First Kiss

> "Of all sad words of tongue and pen, the saddest are these: 'It might have been!'" [8]

She was a much older woman than I and was supposedly experienced in the art of French kissing. Of course, at the pre-teen age of twelve I had no idea what that meant but the better part of being a "Kool Kid" was to fake it. Sharon was 14—really old for the 8th grade—as I recall, and a late bloomer. At the end of the school year, the 8th grade class took a day long trip to someplace exotic. For us, it was the land of Lincoln in Springfield, Illinois, 1964. On the train ride back, Sharon and I sat next to each other holding hands for almost the

---

[8] Charles Eliot, ed. *The Harvard Classics*, V. 42, English Poetry (New York: P. F. Collier & Son Co. 1910), p.1355. These are the concluding lines of a poem by John Greenleaf Whittier (1807-1892) entitled, "Maud Muller." In melancholy verse Whittier tells the tale of two lovers whose passion is only seen, remembered and misunderstood from a distance. Oh, what might have been! (Public Domain).

FIRST KISS

entire time until my buddies made fun of me. Not Kool. Caving into sarcastic peer pressure, I had no choice but to "divorce" her and move back to my seat. So I did. That was the preface to our brief romance but now that school was out and summer had begun I decided it was time to make it up to her.

The bike ride from 54th Damen down to 37th Honore street on Chicago's southside was a feat of stamina and endurance in the summer heat. Dodging cars, trucks and motorcycles I finally made it to the Damen overpass on 47th street. The overpass was a ten block shortcut through the Chicago stockyards which deposited me on the corner of 37th Damen not far from Sharon's neighborhood. I had asked my best buddy Bob to rendezvous with me on our bikes, which we did, and then we went cruising over to Sharon's house.

The first kiss is an explosive moment in a young boy's life. Anticipation, expectation and rejection all collided with one another as I walked up the front porch steps to her house to ring the doorbell. What dumb words would tumble out of my mouth after I rang the bell? Duh, I had no idea. Would she even open the door after the "train-wreck romance" return trip from Springfield? Duh, I had no idea. I pushed the buzzer. I waited. I tried again. After two rings she answered the door. Slowly the door opened, she looked at me with a perky surprised smile and waited for me to speak first.

"Hi, Sharon, how are you doing?"

No response.

"Are you home alone?"

(Ha-ha! What a question for a twelve year old boy to ask! Were my intentions honorable??)

No response, just a pause and with a sly smile she said, "Yep, would you like to come in?"

Paydirt! This was it but I really didn't want to just sit and gab. I wanted to steal a kiss. That was the mission. Meanwhile, my buddy Bob had been circling in the street on his bike riding back and forth watching the mission unfold. I stepped into the doorway. My hands reached for Sharon's waist. I raised my lips toward hers. She moved hesitatingly in my direction. Great ecstasy would soon be mine, joy and bliss sublime! There in the doorway to love's embrace our lips nearly touched.

Crash! Boom! Bang! It was enough to jar anyone loose from the trance of romantic expectations. My buddy Bob in his haste to get the best view of the situation had crashed his bike into the rear bumper of a nearby parked car. He fell off the bike and lay moaning in the street. Sharon, startled, looked away and said, "What happened?" Seeing Bob sprawled out in the street, she started to giggle knowing that his voyeuristic eyes had just crushed the moment.

Our lips never did touch. No kiss, just a sigh. Passion from a distance. Oh, what might have been! I slinked away down the front steps to see how badly hurt Bob was. He wasn't. We both hopped on our bikes and cruised away. My almost first kiss with Sharon was now permanently in my rear view mirror, this time for good. Fickle romance! Maybe the life of a monk was still the best option for me. Only God knows and He wasn't planning on telling me any time soon, at least not yet. His script included a little more impossible squeezing through the eye of the needle and another launch off the flight deck.

The Bike Fight

"A bully is always a coward."[9]

Never underestimate the lifelong impact a good father can have upon his young son. Dad's perennial advice to me growing up on the south side of Chicago was simple and meant to be decisive. One day

---

9   Farlex Dictionary of Idioms. S.v. "bully is always a coward." Retrieved May 24 2023 from https://idioms.thefreedictionary.com/bully+is+always+a+coward

THE BIKE FIGHT

after lunch, he said, "Do you want to know how to stop a bully from bullying you?"

I said, "Sure Dad, tell me how."

He said, "All you have to do is roll up your fingers into a ball (make sure you keep your thumb on the outside, kid), make a fist and whop him a good one right in the nose. It's that simple. It's guaranteed. After that, he won't bother you anymore."

Of course, the part that Dad left out was what if the bully whops you first and you never get in a counter-strike? What then? Run home to Mama? But that was beside the point in Dad's mind. If you really feel threatened, just hit him first. Too bad for me, it didn't quite work out that way the first time.

I had wanted a new bike for some time now that my legs were long enough to reach the pedals of a brand new 26 inch Schwinn bike from Sears & Roebuck's that I had my heart set on. By the time my 10th birthday arrived on a hot August day in Chicago, 1960, Mom and Dad surprised me with a new bike. It had everything I wanted; real chrome fenders, a sharp looking red and white frame, built in head-lights and a horn. And for some snazzy personal glitz,

My brand new Schwinn bike with all the chrome extras from Sears & Roebucks, August 31, 1960

I added handlebar streamers. It was as they use to say in Chicago, "The cat's pajamas!" It was all mine and the envy of the neighborhood and that's when the trouble began.

It's a law of nature that every kid growing up wants more of what every other kid in the neighborhood has. There are no boundaries to envy and jealousy. It can spring into action at the turning of a leaf and so it happened.

I was riding my bike down the narrow alley behind the street of our bungalow homes on south Francisco avenue. Chicago is laid out very logically in a grid network with most every city block divided in half by an alley. Here all the garbage cans were kept to keep the garbage trucks off the main street. Almost every house had a small backyard bounded by a garage that faced the alley. It was the place where kids loved to gather to avoid traffic in the street, play baseball, catch football, play cops and robbers with cap pistols and loiter as a general hang-out.

Time to strut my stuff. I was cruising down the back alley behind our home on my new bike, streamers flying, lights on and my finger poised over the horn button ready to remove any people obstacles in my way. I was looking good. Ahead of me hanging around a neighbor's open garage door was my "sometime" good buddy Willy, and some of his pals. About seven to eight kids in total as I recall. I say "sometime" good buddy because frankly, Willy was a pain in the ass, literally. He had a club foot and wore a special heavy boot and brace on his right foot. Whenever we got to wrestling in the grass he always managed to kick me somehow in the shins or my posterior leaving a decent bruise. He was loud and uncouth. He was raised by a proud Irish Roman Catholic family whose heritage and traditions would always be subject to suspicion from the narrow, conservative Lutheran tradition in which I was brought up. I knew God was on my side; not too sure about his side.

As I approached Willy and his buddies on my bike, I sounded the horn to let me pass. It didn't quite work that way. They surrounded me on my bike causing me to stop in the middle of the alley with Willy leading the charge. Why he was particularly nasty that day, I have no clue. Willy began to shove and push me trying to knock me off my bike, which he did. I had no idea what would happen next but I just

THE BIKE FIGHT

knew that I was in harm's way and my bike was soon to be a crunched fatality. I ran home to Mama crying all the way shouting something about, "My bike! My bike!" Dad, who had spent a good deal of money on my bike, sensed his investment was in jeopardy and was incensed. He ran out of the house in his Tee shirt dragging me along with him to the scene of the crime. Mom followed at a distance.

Dad said to me in front of the gaggle of kids, "Which kid pushed you off your bike?" Word gets out quickly in Chicago when the neighborhood senses a slugfest is about to begin. Just a few minutes had passed since I had been knocked off my bike and already the crowd was swelling in numbers. Moms, Dads, brothers, sisters, and all the typical tough guys had gathered to see the action.

Meekly, I pointed to Willy, tears in my eyes, whimpering and said, "That's the one, Dad, he pushed me off my bike," which bike, by the way, still lay crumpled in the alley. I thought for sure that now I had nailed the criminal Dad would make short work of him. Dad was not a tall guy, five foot three inches at best. But he had a muscular chest and arms and always seemed to project a fearless attitude in the face of danger. I was eager to see Willy get the bruising he deserved! Dad would settle the score once and for all.

Dad said to me, "Mark, go over there and whop him in the nose!" Now sons should always obey the voice of their father especially when it is a voice of reason and wisdom. "Bop him in the nose?" Is that reasonable? Is that wise?? What if he hits me back? What then? I might get hurt!

Dad said it again, "Mark, go over there and whop him in the nose. He was trying to steal your bike."

Saying it a second time didn't add any motivation to fight. So, I stood there holding up my bike with the crooked handlebars and began to cry. There was no way out. To make matters worse everyone in the crowd began to mock me, laugh at me and call me a wimp. I was crushed, hurt and afraid all at the same time. You've got to realize how wimpy and devastated I felt standing beside my strong and aggressive father. Here he was, telling me to get in the fight and he himself was standing all alone in front of a bunch of jeering, mocking neighbors. When a fight breaks out in Chicago, there's no telling how many people will jump in. But Dad was fearless. I suppose that after three and half years in WWII serving in the combat zones of the Mediterranean and the Pacific as a Pharmacist's mate cleaning up the bloody carnage of war, a back alley fight in Chicago was mere child's play.

No, I didn't go over and whop Willy in the nose though he deserved it. I walked my bike home limping along nursing the broken ego of a ten year old boy, whimpering and crying all the way. No fight that day. No back alley justice served just the gnawing feeling that I had let my Dad down. I had embarrassed him. I had not lived up to his expectations of a boy becoming a man. I didn't stand up for myself and he was right. I had been afraid to fight and face the danger. I'm sure Dad was seriously wondering if his middle son would turn out to be a wimp or a man.

It was a tough lesson to swallow for a ten year old kid from Chicago. Looking back, I see clearly now, how on that one hot August day in a Chicago alley many of my future attitudes in life were shaped as the years have rolled by. If a bully is always a coward because he preys on the weak, it certainly appeared to me at the time just the reverse; namely, that Willy was the tough guy and I the coward.

Living up to Dad's expectations would haunt me for a long time. I wanted him to be proud of me not ashamed or embarrassed. Over time, my embarrassment would morph into mature strength but also coupled with some reckless behavior along the way. God's script for my life would squeeze out cowardice and folly and deflate the invincible aura of the bully.

True strength defends the weak and the helpless. It does not attack them. You can learn a lot from a bully, negatively. I had been baptized into Christ Jesus. God had engaged His script for my life. Someday I would learn that the greatest act of bravery in the face of bullies was Christ crucified upon His cross. He shamed them with His love. He overpowered them with His forgiveness. He rose from the dead in spite of their hate and mockery. Bully defeated.

Who are the "bullies" in your life? How and where do they bother you and pester you the most? That is precisely where you must face the bully not with fear and cowardice but with strength and courage through the cross of Christ. Stand like a man, *the* man, Christ Jesus, who is God's script for your life. He is the eye of the needle. He is the safe landing aboard the flight deck of God's grace. He makes the impossible, possible. Dear Lord, launch our faith once again!

The Take Down

"You ain't so bad! You ain't so bad!!"[10]

The Beatles were in. The hair was long and Rock 'n Roll launched a whole new culture with its own language. Tee shirts were tight. Jeans were tighter. Cigarettes were Kool rolled up in your sleeve. Cuban heels finished off the tough guy ensemble.

Long hair was never my thing even when I had a full head of hair. Today, I would just be ecstatic if the back of my head couldn't be seen from the front. Nevertheless, every haircut in those days had to look like you never got a haircut in the first place, just a wee little trim. It was all about maintaining a certain coolness, posture and most of all a non-sissy, tough guy attitude.

We do not choose the earthly environment we are born into, yet where one grows up shapes a kid's personality, style and attitudes for life, for better or for worse. Chicago's south side was a tough neighborhood back in the 50's and 60's but a far cry from the violence that

---

10   Typical southside Chicago challenge.

fills it today. The Chicago I knew and loved is firmly embedded in the memory and recesses of my mind and will probably never dawn again due to the ravishing of so many neighborhoods through drugs, gangs, guns and violence. But I pray that God's extraordinary grace will visit Chicago once again and write a new script for my hometown. With God all things are possible.

In my day, my parents were not terribly concerned if I rode my bike miles from home. As long as I paid attention to my environment, avoided the dangers along the way and returned by dinner time, I was good to go for several hours. When we lived at the 60th South Francisco address, I still attended St. Andrew Lutheran School from the 3rd through the 7th grade. In the 7th grade I would often ride the CTA bus down 59th Street to Damen avenue, transfer busses, and then continue down to 37th Damen. It was about a 25 minute ride, depending on traffic. Sometimes I rode with friends, sometimes alone. No fears. No worries. Just an eleven or twelve year old boy riding the city bus to go to school or get home. The adults around you always looked out after you. But when you disembarked the bus, who knew what new adventure awaited you. The next two block walk to St. Andrew school could be filled with trouble.

Usually, as the St. Andrew kids were walking to school one way, on the other side of the street was a bunch of public school kids walking to their school the other way. More often than not the tough guys in their group would call out across the street toward the "sissies" in our group going to a Christian school. If you stared back at them, the next comment you heard was, "Hey dude, what are you lookin' at? You lookin' at me? Huh, Lookin' for a little action? Chicken?" The trick was not to stare and not to engage. Faking like you never heard the taunt in the first place usually worked, but not always. Such was life going to school every day in Chicago. Danger, bullying and fist fights were never far away. Such an environment created what the military calls "SA" Situational Awareness. Once you've got it, you never lose it.

THE TAKE DOWN

Link the back alley bike fight incident above with the daily walk to school and you can begin to see how important it was for a kid in Chicago to put on a tough guy demeanor because if you looked tough enough from a distance and walked with a bit of a swagger most bullies would not bother you. That was the grade school philosophy and most kids growing up utilized it to avoid a fight. The truth is that most bullies weren't half as tough as they thought they were and, if challenged, their bullying career would come to a smashing halt because they would be publicly shamed by a real tough guy.

Let me illustrate what I mean by a *real* tough guy. In the eighth grade, our principal, Mr. Schlegel, took the entire class to the neighborhood McKinley park gym one afternoon on a school day to watch a basketball tournament. It was always great to get out of school for whatever reason and this day proved to be no exception. The whole class filed into the balcony, spread out on the bleachers and watched the game. Within a few seconds of taking our seats, my SA kicked in and I noticed a group of leather jacketed teens seated across from us about 40 feet away. At first they kept eyeing us to figure out who we were but one of them seemed to be particularly agitated and looking to stir up a little trouble. Apparently, Mr. Schlegel noticed the same thing and when the main bully came strutting over in our direction to cause trouble, Mr. Schlegel intercepted him before he could get close enough to our class to interact with anybody.

"What do you want, son?" Mr. Schlegel said tersely. My first thought was that's a pretty bold statement considering this punk kid was as big as the principal, in a leather jacket and menacing some pretty ugly moves. And then the extraordinary thing happened. Before the tough guy could make his move, Mr. Schlegel spun him around, knocked him to the ground, grabbed the back of his head and headlocked the bully's head between his own legs. In one swift movement, the bully found himself face down, staring at the floor on his knees, "disarmed" and locked between the Principal's kneecaps. Mr. Schlegel grunted in a menacing voice, "Had enough, kid? Now, get back to your seat and mind your own business." It was all over in a blinding flash of male testosterone shot out of excited adrenal glands. Pot-bellied Mr. Schlegel was Kool after all! Who would have known it? Who would have predicted it?

Then and there, it began to dawn upon my twelve-year old brain that being tough is more than just looking tough. Maybe, a whole lot more, like facing danger head-on in order to protect others from the so-called bullies of life. The learning curve of extraordinary grace began to slowly percolate through my pre-teen brain in this human interaction I had just witnessed between the Principal and the take-down of "Mr. Tough Guy"—"You ain't so bad!" God alone makes real tough guys who stand fearlessly for the right. God threads the eye of the needle creating hearts of courage, every time.

Laughter . . . Still the Best Medicine

"A happy heart makes the face cheerful."
Proverbs 15:13

Most every family has their own brand of humor. Few do not. The humor may range from teasing comments to sarcasm to practical jokes to horseplay. How dull life would be without a sense of humor and a knee-slappin' belly burstin' good laugh now and then.

You would think that lovely, sweet, forever kind and generous Grandma Essig (my mother's mother) would not be prone to practical jokes, but she was. After a hard day's work in the 4th grade filled with pencil pushing, arithmetic and pinging spit balls off the back of another kid's head in the row in front of you, Mom had left me with after school instructions to walk down the street to Jim's Finer Foods. It was

LAUGHTER... STILL THE BEST MEDICINE

Jim's Finer Foods

Uncle Jim, my Godfather, and one of the nicest gentlemen you would ever have the privilege to meet.

a small delicatessen that Uncle Jim (my mother's brother) owned on 35th street, about two blocks away from St. Andrew Lutheran school. It was a special treat for me because I could always persuade Uncle LeRoy, (my Mom's younger brother) to serve up a ham sandwich, sliced paper thin and piled high on a Kaiser roll. Everything plain. No fixings just the sweet taste of golden, savory fresh ham on a fresh bakery roll. It was delicious and succulent, as my father was fond of saying.

In the backroom, Uncle Jim kept a German shepherd as a guard dog for the store. The dog was big and sported a beautiful coat of brown and black hair. As you approached the half-door to the backroom you would be rudely awakened by a deep ferocious bark and a large canine straining against a taut chain warning you to step no further. You get the picture.

One day after school while eating one of those delicious ham sandwiches in the backroom of the store at the round break-table, Grandma came in, sat down and we had a pleasant conversation, as always. After she went out to tend the store, I glanced over to my right and noticed something laying on the floor a few feet distant from the dog that didn't look too pleasant. The German shepherd was on a leash tied to the wall and seemingly out of reach of the unpleasant substance. At that moment Uncle LeRoy walked in, stared at the floor, raised his voice and said to me, "Mark, did you do this?"

"Do what, Uncle LeRoy?"

"Leave this mess on the floor?"

"No, of course not! I don't know what you're talking about!"

With great exasperation he said, "If you gotta go, there's the

My sweet Grandma Essig!

bathroom (pointing to the hallway). Do your business there please, and not on the floor!"

I didn't know what to say. What was Uncle LeRoy accusing me of? I know the store's backroom was not the tidiest place but I would never do it on the floor! Civilized south-sider Chicago kids are all potty trained by the 4th grade. Who would do such a thing? With that, Uncle LeRoy, bent down and picked up the offending mess, threw it in the trash, and stormed out of the backroom. He then waited on some customers while I devoured my succulent ham sandwich and drink in order to get the heck out of the store.

A couple of minutes later, my sweet, little ol' Grandma came waltzing in, sat down beside me and picked up our conversation where she left off. A moment later Uncle LeRoy returned, gave me a suspicious look, went over to the backroom sink, washed his hands and went back up front to wait on another customer.

When Grandma left the second time, I was horrified to see another unpleasant mess lying on the backroom floor in about the same spot from the last clean-up. I didn't know what to do. The first incident could be written off to a bystander as an unfortunate slip but the second? No sooner had my boyish mind begun to contemplate what I might say next if accused when Uncle LeRoy burst back into the back room, spied the unsightly mess on the floor, grabbed a towel to pick it up, looked at me and said, "Awe, com 'on, Mark, if you gotta go to the bathroom, go! But for heaven's sake don't do it on the floor. What did you do this time, shake it out of your pants leg?"

Well, you can just image my chagrined face glowing crimson red. "What are you talking about, Uncle LeRoy. I didn't do anything! Believe me!"

Adults rarely believe kids then or now. Kids are always in denial about their behavior and the real truth lies somewhere in between. The half-door to the backroom swung open again and Grandma returned to the scene of the crime, sat down next to me and tried to console me. "It's OK, Mark, we all have bathroom troubles from time to time. I've got some medicine you can take to ease your bowel problems. Would you like some?"

Uncle LeRoy was still cleaning up the mess behind Grandma's back when, as he started to exit the backroom, I noticed something out of the corner of my eye go rolling across the floor and coming to a stop in the same conspicuous place of the last accident. The dog was still on a leash and sleeping so it couldn't be from him. I got up from my chair in the middle of Grandma's prescription advice and took a few steps toward the offending mess, bending over for a closer inspection. I said, "Is that for real? Where did it come from??"

The gig was up. You could hear LeRoy laughing all the way from the front of the store. LeRoy had tears in his eyes he was laughing so hard and Grandma just giggled like a big bowl of wiggly Jell-O. The joke was on me. The offending mess was rubberized dog poop and Uncle LeRoy's latest adventure in his bag of tricks. Uncle LeRoy said to me, "You should have seen the look on your face, Mark! It was worth a million bucks!"

Maybe so, I wouldn't doubt it. It took a few moments for my deep chagrin to turn to nervous laughter but it did. Before the unveiling of the practical joke, I was half-convinced that I had a bowel problem, so it was with great relief that my name was cleared and my good health restored. Shortly after that, I had to go to the bathroom. Apparently, in the mundane unveiling of our ordinary days, God's script also contains the funny section.

Old Days

> "Why were the former days better than these?"
> *Ecclesiastes 7:10*

> "To everything there is a season.
> A time for every purpose under heaven."
> *Ecclesiastes 3:1*

Old days filled with memories, bright, long, fresh and crisp, are etched into my mind. Longfellow was right, the thoughts of youth are long, long thoughts.[11] Grade school summers in Chicago from June to

---

11   Charles Eliot, ed. *The Harvard Classics*, V. 42, English Poetry (New York: P. F. Collier & Son Co. 1910) p. 1290. (Public domain). Solomon once wrote, "A word fitly spoken is like apples of gold in settings of silver." Proverbs 25:11. Longfellow's poem entitled, "My Lost Youth," in my opinion fits the proverb admirably. The selection of words, flow, meter and rhyme of Longfellow's poetry dances lightly on the ear when spoken out loud and warms the heart when read. Here are two selected verses from "My Lost Youth."

> Often I think of the beautiful town, that is seated by the sea.
> Often in thought go up and down, the pleasant streets of that dear town, and my youth comes back to me. And a verse of a Lapland song is haunting my memory still, "A boy's will is the wind's will, and the thoughts of youth are long, long thoughts."

> There are things of which I may not speak, there are dreams that cannot die.
> There are thoughts that make the strong heart weak,
> and bring a pallor into the cheek, and a mist before the eye.
> And the words of that fatal song come over me like a chill,
> "A boy's will is the wind's will, and the thoughts of youth are long, long thoughts."

> It's a pity that such poetry is not read nor sought out in our classrooms today. It is not the number of books that makes a life rich in thought, word and deed but rather selected good

OLD DAYS

September seemed to last forever. The main task every morning was to figure out what you wanted to do and who you wanted to play with today while carefully avoiding all household chores before you disappeared into the neighborhood. The chore-avoidance strategy seldom worked with my parents but in my case it seemed that my older brother Neil got the lion's share of chores of which he often complained. Nice to be the middle kid and Mom's "favorite!" To grow up on the south side of Chicago in the 50s and 60s was to be born into a world bursting with a million boyish adventures. Here are a few snippets from my memory book reminiscent of a boy's life on the southside of old Chicago:

The scattered vacant lots throughout the city were often overgrown with weeds and piles of dirt which we turned into racing trails for our bikes. The same vacant lots provided an ample supply of insects, spiders, grasshoppers and caterpillars who soon became the inhabitants of a homemade screened-in cardboard box museum. Grasshoppers were especially fun, known scientifically as chewing herbivorous insects. If you held the grasshopper for a few seconds in your hand closing your fingers around it but not crushing it, it would spit brown "tobacco" juice into your hand. Really Kool! Rarely did that stop us from taking the next bite out of a candy bar we had been munching on with the same hand. No time for personal hygiene in the midst of play while building a grasshopper museum.

Tossing the bat to pick captains for a "sandlot" baseball game was the local custom. The three finger rule prevailed. If you could squeeze in your last three fingers just below the top of the bat handle—*Whamo!*—you were the winner and the first to pick sides for your team. Softball was played with a 16 inch softball in those days called

books, read over again and again for their inspiration, depth and perspective in the passing of our days. Some of my best friends are books! Words, fitly spoken, are gifts of God that adorn the footprints of our lives. Words, good words, feed and nourish our souls.

the "clincher," a favorite Chicago softball game with unique historical Chicago roots. The ball is 16 inches in circumference and played without a glove, at least it was in my day.

A brand new softball was quite hard and stung sharply when caught in your bare hands. It was another Chicago sissy-test to see if you would cry or not when fielding a hard-struck ball smacked in your direction. Usually, I played 3rd base, occasionally shortstop. More than once, I caught a hard hit ball flying down the 3rd base line and I didn't cry, (whimper yes!) but no tears. Simply remarkable for a "man" twelve years of age, don't you think?

After the 4th of July, the Chicago street gutters were a cornucopia of spent fireworks. On the morning of the 5th we would scour all the gutters in the neighborhood for blocks, searching for duds and how to relight them without injury. Every kid had his own unique relighting technique. It was always a vigorous discussion among the boys. No injuries that I recall. No missing fingertips relighting spent dud firecrackers. The grace of God prevails even over the dumb things young boys will so often do.

Run, run, run! Everybody moved fast in Chicago. We use to play "Tag. You're it!" It was a game that would cover the whole city block. The last kid tagged had to count out loud to a hundred while everyone else scattered up and down the block seeking cover. We hid behind cars, in gangways, and behind bushes. There, under cover, you waited for the precise moment when you would leap from your hiding place and race back to the fire hydrant which was positioned in the middle of the block before the leader could catch you. Touching the hydrant, you shouted out, "Olee, Olee, Ocean Free!"[12] Whatever the heck that meant, I have no idea. In Chicago, eight city blocks make up a mile. A single city block

---

12   The Toledo version where Connie, the love of my life, grew up was: "Alee, Alee, Oxen free!" Personally, I think the Chicago version is more macho and sounds much *kooo-ler!*

is 660 feet long or 220 yards from corner to corner. The race to the fire hydrant was often a 50 yard dash or greater. The game usually lasted for an hour. It was no wonder nobody gained weight as a kid regardless of how much junk food he or she had eaten all day long. All of our fun was outdoors and the running never stopped.

Dad loved to play golf. I wouldn't say he was a great golfer but he had some great moments in the sport. Marquette park golf course was about a mile from our house on South Francisco avenue. Often, Jerry (my neighborhood buddy down the street) and I would hop on our bikes in the early morning hours carrying a bag of golf clubs over our shoulder and ride to Marquette park. It was a 9 hole public golf course (still there today) kept in reasonably good condition considering all the traffic that rampaged its fairways. Your first tee shot was off a rubber mat, straightaway, about 370 yards. The right side of the fairway was lined with cars parked along the street that meandered and encircled Marquette park. It was always great fun to see if any golfer would slice his tee shot into the parked cars. More than once you would hear a loud ping, then the sound of broken glass followed by the golf ball bouncing down the street ricocheting off doors, bumpers and chrome grills.

On one such occasion, I sliced my tee shot perfectly into a bunch of parked cars and then watched my ball keep rolling out-of-bounds down the street. Because there were always a bunch of impatient guys lined up behind you and waiting to play next, you weren't allowed to take a second shot from the tee. The standing orders were, "Just grab your cart, son, retrieve your ball and move on." Where your golf ball exited the fairway out of bounds, the golf rules state that you drop another ball in place at that exit point, take a penalty stroke and swing again. In my case, I was hoping that maybe my ball would have kicked back into the fairway further up the street so I kept walking forward. Sure enough, I found my golden tee shot had rolled about 200 yards down the street and ended up out of bounds in the nearby gutter. With one deft move oblivious to all onlookers, I kicked the ball back into the fairway, nailed a short approach shot to the green, two putted and holed out.

Later that day, I bragged to Dad about my 300 yard drive and paring the first hole. He was simply incredulous or at least he appeared that way. "What a golf shot for a twelve year old boy!" he exclaimed. "300 yards! Wow! Maybe someday, Mark, you will make me rich and I can retire early!" I had no idea what kind of profit-sharing plan Dad had in mind but it tickled my eardrums. Of course, Dad knew, having played Marquette park himself what had happened, but for the moment, it was a good golf yarn stretching a 100 hundred yard bad slice into a 300 yard monster drive. "Great shot, son!" Dad said with a nod of his head, and I was smart enough to smile, keep my mouth shut and leave it alone at that.

On the corner of 79th and Western Avenue near my cousin Charley's neighborhood, use to be a huge 40 acre prairie, a veritable treasure trove of delights for young boys on bikes to discover and explore. One lone tree graced this prairie field, as I recall, to which we quickly cut a bicycle path and built a tree house out of discarded lumber, broken sheets of plywood, cardboard boxes, hammer and nails. No one could enter our tree fort without a password (which changed daily and was often forgotten) or they would be met with warning shots of spitballs, rubber band slingshots and verbal insults hurled from the boy tree dwellers.

I remember numerous sleep-overs at cousin Charlie's house on Artesian avenue, listening to White Sox double-header ball games late into the night. The sound of train whistles, engine calls, and the clanking and coupling of train cars was just a couple of blocks distant from the bedroom window. The sound of the train yards filled the night time air into the wee hours of the morning. There is nothing like train whistles to soothe a young boy's mind to sleep.

It was 1959. Transistor radios were in, Bazooka Joe bubble gum plumped and swelled our cheeks. We looked like we had the mumps. Baseball cards were a quickly growing fad. Trading Luis Aparicio, Minnie Minosa or Nellie Fox for Mickey Mantle or Roger Maris was always a tricky and contested bartering game. Two for one? Three for one? Two for Three? "Awe, com'on. Just gimme the card!" Some baseball cards are worth a lot of money today. Yesterday, they were easy to be found. Who knows where mine went.

Hockey is a great winter sport. It seemed that every winter the lagoon at Marquette Park surrounding the golf course would freeze over for at least a couple of months. If the snow had not been too heavy the night before there would be multiple hockey rinks that could be carved out. Picking up a hockey game on any given wintry Saturday was a simple task. There were always multiple skaters on the ice slapping a puck around with sticks. The hockey sticks were usually hung together by more black electrical tape than wood. Few kids had shin guards which meant that any shot that lifted off the ice made everybody duck for cover real quick. Getting hit in the shin with a flying hockey puck would bring instant tears, a nasty bruise and a scream to your lips (and probably a few choice words). Because the lagoon had many bay-like curves and the two foot raised embankment served excellently as a wall, you had a near perfect hockey rink carved out by nature. However, because the lagoon encircled the park and was wide open at certain points, there was always one side of your home-made hockey rink that opened out into clear ice running for a hundreds of yards. This was a problem, a big problem. When you made your gallant charge down the ice to score a goal and passed the puck to your buddy, if he missed it—as was usually the case—the game would stop and the puck would go sailing forth down a sheet of ice for a hundred yards. Who would get it? Was it a bad pass or a lousy catcher? Arguments ensued, then some rough housing and finally someone would slowly skate away into the distance to retrieve the puck. The game would start up again and last for a few minutes until the next errant pass or catch was attempted but it was still all good solid fun.

After acquiring some hockey gear one year; namely, shin guards, gloves, a jersey and after a long day at the park it was time to hop on a bus and go home. Cousin Charley was with me. As we walked to the bus stop from the lagoon, he walked above the pedestrian bridge, and I skated underneath the bridge. For whatever reason the ice under the bridge did not freeze solid like the rest of the lagoon. The ice cracked and down I went. Briefly, the thought occurred to me, "I wonder how deep this water is?" I still had all my hockey gear on and the extra weight would have deposited me on the bottom of the lagoon with the catfish where I probably would have been discovered preserved in pristine hockey condition sometime next Spring.

The icy water under the bridge was only chest high, thank God. I called out for Charlie who quickly returned and offered me his hockey stick. I thanked him for the gesture but said I'd really like to get out of here now. "Grab the stick!" he said. So I did. He yanked and pulled, I crawled and squirmed until I reached the bank and could drag myself out. It was probably 20 degrees outside. It was freezing cold. I was wet from my neck down. We walked to the bus stop. We waited for the CTA bus. Finally, cold and shivering, the bus arrived. I got home and lived to play another game of hockey. Once again, God's extraordinary grace plucked me out of the icy shallow waters just in time through the extended hockey stick of cousin Charley. It was a moment of God's unsuspecting providential love which trapped me by the tailhook of His grace on His celestial flight deck. Safe, again.

Football. My kind of game. What kid growing up does not love the smell of a good leather football? I distinctly remember one Christmas morning finding a new football under the tree with my name on it. Sheer delight! That night in bed, I curled up with my pillow and my new football beside my head. The smell of fresh leather quickly induced deep REM sleep waves and multiple fantasies about superb broken field running, bruising tackles and spectacular end-zone catches. I was a grid iron hero. The roar of the crowd simply deafening! What amazing football fireworks I dreamt at only ten years of age.

High school tackle football was on my horizon, four years of it, to be exact. What glory, what success, what honor would soon be mine for a speedy half-back? Not much, I'm afraid. A few good plays here and there and a touchdown but it was all offset by bruising charley-horses, a broken knuckle, and a sprained ankle. Still I played well enough to letter in both High School football and wrestling. I was fast, real fast, clocking in at 10.4 seconds in the 100 yard dash with full gear on. Such sweat and sacrifices just to impress the girls! It was all part of the tough guy persona.

The football kid from the southside of Chicago

"*Duh Bears!*" made it to the Super Bowl only once, 1986, where they crushed the New England Patriots 46-10 but they were the NFL champs in 1963 before the merger of the leagues. The Bears have more players enshrined in the NFL football Hall of Fame than any other team including famous half-backs like Gale Sayers and Walter Payton.

At a Armed Forces Exhibition game in the summer of 1966, Cousin Charlie and I watched Sayers strut his stuff as the latest addition to the Chicago backfield. The play that I remember well was a pitch-out to Sayers running to his left up field where he was met by a wall of tacklers. It looked like he wouldn't gain a yard, but the Kansas

Comet, reversed course, circled back behind the quarterback and ran up the other side of the field through several broken tackles gaining 20 to 30 yards on a play where most half-backs would have been down for the count. Sayers could cut and reverse so quickly that the defense would "tackle" Sayers where he used to be just a moment ago. He was absolutely thrilling to watch. Every time he got his hands on the football you expected something big to happen, and it usually did.

Chicago loves football. I was no exception. Your environment growing up shapes your heart and mind, your loves, your hates, your likes and your dislikes. No doubt about it.

Wrestling is a great sport. Unlike football where all the glory on the field is shared by 10 other players whenever a score is made, wrestling is a single man sport. You get all the credit if you win; if you lose, there is no one else to blame. It's a great thrill when during a match you flip your opponent on to his back trying to pin his shoulders to the mat while all your fellow students and team mates are shouting from the bleachers, "Pin! Pin! Pin!"

After one particular match when our wrestling team went to a local restaurant one of the girls from my high school said to me with flirtatious admiration in her eyes, "I really like the way you wrestle!" Now there's a shot in the arm. Wrestling is a girl magnet! Nobody ever said that to me after a football game. I wrestled all four years in high school, the last three at Luther High School South, 87th Kedzie Avenue. I did quite well and was undefeated my last year but not without an apparent misfortune. Here enters the script of God and His extraordinary grace, a single footstep that would change the future course of my life, life pierced again by God's needle of grace in the tapestry of life He had woven for me.

During my last year of high school after I had wrestled every opponent in my weight class in the PSL[13] once and half-way through the

---

13   The membership of the Private School League in Chicago included about 8 high schools in total, as I recall.

1967-68 season I cracked a couple of vertebrae in my lower back during a practice wrestling match against a much heavier team mate in the 182 lb. weight class. My weight class was 145 lb. I was sure my back would heal in a couple of weeks but Dr, Gareiss, our family Doctor, after taking a couple of X-rays said, "No more wrestling for you, son, unless you want to make it worse and possibly paralyze yourself from the waist down." I was unconvinced but that was enough for Mom and Dad. Game over. Reluctantly, very reluctantly, I turned in my uniform and head gear. I was bummed out but the sports curse turned out to be a disguised hidden blessing of grace unawares and another footprint revealed from the script of God.

On December 1, 1969, the nation held its first Vietnam Draft Lottery since WWII. All selectees would be chosen by birthday. All young men born between January 1st, 1944 and December 31st, 1950 would be eligible. My birthday, August 31st, 1950, fit in just nicely.

366 blue plastic balls containing every birthday tumbled randomly in a glass container. Each draw held the future fate for every potential draft selectee. Lucky me. August 31st was chosen early in the lottery. I was number 11. In that year, 1969, all eligible males in sequence up to the number 195 were drafted and inducted. It meant I would soon receive a letter from Uncle Sam in the mail, and I did.[14]

On a cold wintry December morning at "zero-dark-thirty" just two weeks later I found myself at a downtown Chicago recruiting and examination station. Just because you receive a notice from the draft board doesn't mean the next step is to issue you a uniform. First you must be thoroughly examined from head to toe. Communicable

---

14   I had changed colleges that Fall from Western Illinois University, Macomb, Illinois, which ran classes on a quarterly system to Northern Illinois University, Dekalb, Illinois, which ran classes on a semester system. This meant that when I changed colleges, I was not enrolled in class from Thanksgiving, 1968, until January, 1969, thus losing my student deferment at the very time the lottery was conducted thus making me eligible immediately for the draft. The reason for changing colleges? Macomb, Illinois was 230 miles and 3.5 hours away by car from my girlfriend's home in the western suburbs of Chicago. On the other hand, Dekalb, Illinois, was only 50 miles away and 1 hour by car. I owned no car in college but I knew the art of hitchhiking a ride. My choice, my script, so I thought and believed.

diseases would disqualify you especially VD, along with hernias, hemorrhoids, physical deformities and a host of other conditions.

The exam room was huge. There we stood in our underwear in parallel lines of 50. "Drop your drawers to your ankles, bend over and turn around!" the Doc shouted. "Spread your cheeks!" was the next embarrassing command. Together with his assistant they went up and down the aisles checking every bent-over rear end for a bad case of hemorrhoids and anything else they could find. Imagine having that job and trying to sleep at night. About 200 guys were processed that single day; about six were rejected. All six, I believe, had Doctor's letters. I was one of the six. A letter from Dr. Gareiss plus a few X-rays indicated that I had a couple of hairline fractures in two lower vertebrae from high school wrestling. It was enough for Uncle Sam to disqualify me on the spot.

The 60's were turbulent years in America. I was no draft-dodger. I was prepared to serve my country like my Navy Dad in WWII and my Navy Grampa Schreiber in WWI but Uncle Sam didn't want a healthy 19 year old kid with a weak lower back and that was final. What snapped in my back on the high school wrestling mat during practice that December day in 1967 was sufficient to disqualify me for the draft two years later in 1969. It was God's script in action once again which did not include a launch into the jungles of Vietnam.

Think for a moment just how different life would have been had I been drafted that day and served in Vietnam. PTSD and moral injury might be my lasting legacy to this day, let alone loss of life or limb. Or, I might have been adorned with a chest full of combat medals for bravery and valor and given a hero's welcome. Either way, my worldview and perspective on many issues would have been intensely painted by Vietnam. But it was not to be, all because I cracked a couple of vertebrae in high school wrestling two years earlier.

Linkage? At the time I saw little divine linkage but age and a few more years in life brings vivid clarity. God's script for my life did not include Vietnam. His extraordinary grace had another mission for me to follow that would soon be launched from the flight deck of His heavenly grace.

Luck, you say? Mere fortuitous coincidence? I think not. Your baptism into Christ comes with a 100% iron clad guarantee. "All things work together for good to those who love God, to those who are called according to His purpose." Romans 8:28. You, the reader, have probably been baptized by water into Christ either in infancy or later in life. Probably greater than 80% of all Americans today can claim this same heritage. But if you never recall your Baptism, if you see no linkage between your Baptism and the daily events of your life, then you are discounting your Baptism, even despising it.

Baptism into Christ Jesus is a covenant between God and you. The good news is that God will always keep His covenant towards you even though we may despise, neglect and forget it. The goodness of God over all of your life is planned to lead you back to repentance and keep you there. It is the essence of His extraordinary grace toward you and His evidence is everywhere in your life. God knows what He is doing and He is doing it well all the time, all for you. Of this I am absolutely certain. Timing is everything in life.

Over time, my back healed. Eleven years later, I passed the qualifying physical exam and was commissioned a Naval Officer, Ensign, Chaplain Corps, May 9th, 1980, fit for duty to serve God and Country. I would serve with the Navy/Marine Corps team for the next 25 years until 2005. In addition to an exciting and superb Chaplain Corps ministry, I can add a proud footnote to my career. I never failed to score less than first class on every Navy and/or Marine Corps biannual physical fitness test in my entire career. God blesses. God heals. His grace is simply extraordinary.

When God launched you off the bow of His flight deck you were certain you knew your own destiny. You had your life's mission all planned out but you boltered again and again during your dance of life. Next time around you were trapped, landing safely on the flight deck of His good grace. There you paused, reflected and began to understand that God's script must of necessity overpower your script, your timing and your ambitions whether you want it or not. The first steps of faltering trust were beginning to appear in your heart and mind.

Is it good or bad to reminisce? Is it God-pleasing or just warmed over nostalgia with a dash of melancholy to keep your mind forever locked in the past?[15] It all depends. "On what?" you ask. Your motive, I assert. If your motive is to relive the past and wish you could go back to yesteryear when the days of your life seemed to be so much better than you can imagine, you are foolish to do so. The only good motive is to discern the pattern of His handiwork in your earthly days, to recognize His protective steadfast love, to rejoice and give Him the thanks due His name. This is the right motive and doing so will strengthen your thanksgiving toward God today, in the present moment, immensely.[16]

Any other motive will rust your brain, tarnish your thinking and turn you eventually into a cynical, bitter grumpy old man or woman forever whining about all the bad choices you once made thinking that nothing can undo your past. Therein lies the mental trap of eternal grumpiness. You have forgotten. God's script is better than your script. His choices for your life correct and realign the choices you have so carefully made for yourself. In fact, God's script overwhelms and corrects your script. Learn to think rightly about this extraordinary grace bestowed upon you since the day you were baptized.

I have only one question. Have you landed safely on the flight deck of God's grace yet or are you still searching for the "meatball" on the horizon?

---

15 "For who knows what is good for man while he lives the few days of his vain life, which he passes like a shadow? For who can tell man what will be after him under the sun?" Eccl. 6:12.
16 The Savior said, "No man having put his hand to the plough and looking back is fit for the kingdom of God." Luke 9:62. Absolutely true but it must harmonized with, "I remember the days of old. I meditate on all Your works. I muse on the works of Your hands." Psalm 143:5. Surely God's extraordinary grace lived out in any ordinary life creates a long list of wonderful faith-filled memories to strengthen the heart in future days of sorrow or darkness. No contradiction here in the Word of God just beautiful harmony.

Footprints of Sorrow

"Like cold water to a thirsty soul, so is good news from a far country."

Proverbs 25:25

My older brother Neil, by four years, joined the Marine Corps in the Spring of 1964 before finishing his senior year at Lindblom High School on Chicago's southside.[17] Neil was 17. I was 13. The minimum recruiting age for the Corps was 18 so Dad had to sign for him. Neil had joined the ROTC team during his High School years at Lindblom and had won several competitions for expert rifle marksmanship. Good eyes, steady hands. But when Neil joined the Corps, he was running from trouble, girl trouble. I wouldn't learn the whole story until years later.

Marine Corps boot camp has the power to produce real repentance on a variety of subjects under the screaming tutelage of the Drill Instructor and thereby rearrange a person's entire worldview. Boot camp is designed to break you down, get out all that civilian crap, and build you up into a true fighting Marine. The Marines were good at it, real good. In the process they instilled in the recruit strong values of God and country, right from wrong and respect for authority. Our parents are our first God-given authority figures in our life. Sometimes kids disrespect and abuse this precious gift of God. Boot camp gave Neil a change of heart on the subject. Here is a portion of Neil's first letter to me while still in boot camp containing the following brotherly advice and his new outlook on life:

---

17 Lindblom High School, 6130 S. Wolcott Avenue, Chicago, Illinois is the public school Neil attended and joined the ROTC. He received numerous first place awards for expert rifle marksmanship during many high school competitions.

I am proud of you Mark, you did well, you are a good boy, not like me at all. Be good, study, work hard and don't hurt Mom and Dad. I've done that enough. Don't get me wrong, I love the USMC. It's just that I made a lot of mistakes and broke a lot of hearts trying to get in and now I regret them. But that doesn't change them, does it? All I have to say is, "Take the example set by your big brother and do the exact opposite and you will be OK . . . Listen to Mom and Dad always and remember they're the only ones we've got so treat them good, better than I did, and don't fight with Paul for the same reasons."[18]

When Neil joined the Corps the family had moved from my favorite Chicago address on south Francisco avenue to the corner of 54th Damen where Mom and Dad owned and operated two separate businesses. Dad, on the west side of Damen, ran the Delicatessen with a meat market where he personally cut all meat selections for the customer. Mom, on the east side of Damen, ran the dry cleaners. We were a two business family and we lived directly behind the cleaners in a small apartment flat.

Neil loved the Corps and most everything about it especially learning to fire various arms and weapons systems. What he didn't count on nor did Mom and Dad was the Vietnam war. When Neil joined the Corps[19] Vietnam was just starting to get hot. His initial assignment was near the Da Nang US Air Base, 1964. Throughout the war Da Nang was a key air base for the war effort. Early in the war, more than 2500 sorties flew daily mission and bombing raids from Da Nang. Da Nang air base was frequently targeted with mortars and rockets by the VC. I remember Neil telling me that there was no warning when the VC lobbed the first rockets into the camp in the middle of the night, most

---

18   Written from boot camp, MCRD, San Diego, CA, on a Friday evening just before standing guard duty on base, June 12, 1964. Paul is my younger brother by nine years. Just the right size for an older brother to pick on!

19   Neil served two tours of combat in Vietnam during his four year hitch from 1964-1968.

every night. The only warning was the first blast and if it didn't kill you, you raced to the bunker for cover before the next blast and then waited out the attack. So much for a good night's sleep.

During the summer of '65 the evening news stateside cranked up its coverage of the war flooding American TV sets with images of Americans wounded and in body bags. Day after day in 1965, the news and casualty count from Vietnam intensified. The strain on Mom's face was clearly visible.

One particular evening that summer, around 5:30 PM, the evening news broadcasted a special news announcement about heavy enemy activity and fierce firefights near the Da Nang US air base where Neil was stationed on the perimeter. Mom was making dinner for us when Walter Cronkite appeared on our TV screens and described the event with real time footage. At just that moment, Mom collapsed on the kitchen floor in grief. She was sure her firstborn son was dead and if somehow he did manage to make it, he would be wounded and broken for life. I ran over to help her and called Dad. As I recall Mom "rested" in troubled, anxious silence in her bedroom for the rest of the evening.

Neil returned from Vietnam in 1968 after his second tour of combat. He bore no physical wounds of war. This was good news from a far country but the trauma, stress, nightmares and moral injury that followed 'Nam would haunt him for the rest of his life. Neil had been baptized into Christ Jesus in infancy, just like me. The Lord kept His covenant with my brother and granted him 70 earthly years of life, a beautiful, caring and supportive wife, Darlene, three children and grandchildren.

The footprints God had given Neil for the script of his life contained much joy over the years but I would be less than honest if I did not say that there were also many, heart-breaking footprints of sorrow that Mom and Dad, Neil and Dar would walk through life together. Now all four are united, safely trapped by the tailhook of God's love upon the flight deck of God's eternal grace enjoying each other's company perfectly in the heavenly city of God.

The Runaway

> "Life . . . struts and frets his hour upon the stage, and then is heard no more; It is a tale told by an idiot, full of sound and fury, signifying nothing."
>
> *William Shakespeare*[20]

You would think that a younger brother would listen to his older brother's advice and not hurt his parents, wouldn't you? After all, shouldn't we learn from other people's mistakes? Wasn't Vietnam more than enough for Mom and Dad to bear? Even though I was the middle kid and Mom's favorite, I managed to her hurt big time. Looking back my behavior was just pure insanity.

In the summer of 1967, I ran away from home on a motorcycle. It was a Honda Sport 90. Top speed going downhill behind a semi tractor-trailer caught up in his back draft was 58 mph. I had purchased it for less than a hundred bucks. I hid my bike in my buddy's garage a couple of blocks down the street from our home on Winchester street off 85th and Damen avenue.

The reason for leaving home? You guessed it, girl trouble. No, nobody was pregnant I just had issues with the opposite sex. So I figured it was time to start a new life somewhere out in California, probably near the Haight-Ashbury district where free love, free food and free whatever was picking up a head of steam. Today we call it the nerve center of the 60's counter-culture movement; back then, it was just a fantasized utopia, a flawed man-made paradise on earth where all authority could be bucked and you could do or smoke whatever you wanted.

---

20 Charles Eliot, ed. *The Harvard Classics*, V. 46, English Poetry (New York: P. F. Collier & Son Co. 1910), p.388. Act 5, Scene 5. Spoken by Macbeth upon learning the death of Lady Macbeth. *Macbeth* is a tale of the woes that follow damnable ambition scripted with murder on Macbeth's path to claim and secure the throne of the King of Scotland.

THE RUNAWAY

I left a note on my pillow, slipped out my bedroom window undetected early that August Sunday morning, and ran two blocks over to my buddy's garage to get my motorcycle, crank up my machine and take off. (Neil was still serving with the Marines in Vietnam.) I packed a sleeping bag, some clothes, some food and Neil's Ka-bar knife that he had left home during his last furlough just in case I needed to open a can of beans or something. Off I went.

I was 16. It was drizzling lightly. For the next four hours I got lost and made a huge loop of the south Chicago area and suburbs ending up just about where I started. It was noon. Now what to do?? It was still raining. I was soaked and dirty but afraid to go home and face Mom and Dad so I took off again and by evening I had made it to St. Louis, Missouri about 300 miles away. I had only a hundred bucks on me, as I recall, and I didn't want to waste it. It's a long way to California by motorcycle even if food and gas were cheap. I pulled off the road, found a hill above the interstate with no homes nearby, shut down my bike and walked it uphill. At the top, I laid the bike down in the grass. I pulled out my sleeping bag and crawled inside. I was tired, weary, dirty and smelly but took a moment to gaze above at a starred filled night sky wondering what the future would now hold.

When I woke up in the morning, my sleeping bag was covered with dozens of daddy-longleg spiders and other creepy-crawly bugs. I sat up and to my surprise I had parked myself on the top of a hill overlooking a major clover-leaf intersection that was clogged with traffic, exhaust fumes and blaring horns. I was about as hidden as an outhouse in the middle of the road with the door wide open. I managed to shake off the bugs, roll up the sleeping bag, clean up my greasy face and roll the bike down the hill. I started my bike, slipped into traffic and off I went crawling along at 4 mph moving westward in the St. Louis morning traffic.

It was Monday, day two of my runaway adventure. When I finally exited the St. Louis traffic I began to make real progress going west on

Interstate 70. In those days, like seat-belts, it was extremely un-Kool to wear a helmet. Looking like the tough guy I thought I was, I needed no helmet for protection, so I reasoned. The problem with my thinking is that driving a motorcycle on the streets of Chicago is much different than on the wide open interstate where bugs abound, I mean BIG bugs. You know what your windshield looks like after an interstate trip, now you can imagine what my face and forehead looked like. When a bug hits your face at 55 mph it not only leaves its bug body residue all over your skin, it craters a sizeable indentation. Sun glasses spared my eyes but my cheeks and forehead looked like a peperoni pizza left out in the sun too long.

Mile after mile, I drove, unrepentant to stop and consider the pain I was causing back home. I was free (from what I had no idea) but now this moody teenager was actually doing what everyone else was just talking about in my peer group. The adventure of a new life of my own making had just begun and I was going to write its script. From now on I would be the Captain of my own fate and destiny. Kool, Kooler, Koolest!

I crossed half the entire state of Kansas that day and was about 700 miles from home Monday afternoon when flashing blue lights appeared in my rear-view mirror. Politely, I pulled over to the right lane to let the officer pass by. He didn't. He slowed down behind me clicked on his loudspeaker and told me to pull over. At that very moment I heard the voice of God in the back of my head say, "This is it, Mark, game over, end of the road. You will go no farther today."

When the officer went through my belongings and spotted the Ka-bar knife, he asked where I got it. I gave him some lame answer which I'm sure he didn't believe. He directed me into the back of the police car and off we went to the Salina county jail. I thought I would probably be questioned and when they were satisfied that I had done no wrong, I would be released on my own cognizance. Another lame assumption. When they swung the jail door open and ordered me inside

THE RUNAWAY

I had no idea how long I would be staying in my new "home."

Apparently, my folks had called the police on Sunday back in Chicago and had given them a missing person's report. The police officer who pulled me over on the interstate on Monday did so because I fit the description my folks had given the Chicago police. The Salina police office called my Dad with the news. I spent Monday night in jail.

It's about 700 miles from Chicago to Salina, Kansas. As soon as Dad got the news, he drove the entire distance non-stop all Monday night. He arrived Tuesday afternoon while I was sitting in the jail cell. Dad sat down and talked with the police sergeant, conversing intently for some time but out of the range of my hearing.

I had been laying on the top bunk of the jail cell staring at the ceiling. It's hard to describe what I felt the moment I heard the rattle of the keys in the officer's hand, the click of the lock in the jail door and the jail door swing open on its steel hinges. Dad entered the cell. He looked up at me and said, "Come on, Mark, it's time to go home." The full realization of what I had just done, the stupidity of it all, the pain, grief and worry I had caused Mom and Dad was more than I could bear. I hugged Dad; he hugged me. Dad said, "Come on, let's get out of here and get a good steak somewhere." And so we did. Dad rented a hotel room for the night and called Mom from the room. When I heard Mom's worried and weepy voice, I cried like a baby. How could I be so cruel to my own parents after all the love and joy they had given me all the days of my life? How was it possible to be so hard-hearted toward the two people on earth who loved me the most? I don't know. I just don't know. Sin is insanity.

The last thing on my mind in those teenage years was to follow God's footprints and seek out His script for my life. Of His grace, I was unawares. It was all about me, me doing my own thing, and to heck with anyone else. What I created that day were footprints of sorrow that left Mom and Dad wondering what they had done wrong raising their "favorite" middle child. They hurt. I hurt.

When Dad and I finally got back home to Chicago, Mom, Dad and I had a long talk. No harsh judgmental words fell upon me, no painful words of criticism, no berating and no statement like, "How could you have done this to me?" There was just forgiveness, real love and thanking God I was alright. I was home, safe at last. Over time, the footprints of sorrow that I had created by stubbornly following my own narcissistic script would heal and be erased.

Amazingly, as the years rolled by, the runaway middle son episode was never brought up again. When the subject surfaced obliquely in a casual conversation many years later, all that Mom could remember was that Neil was the runaway, not Mark, not my favorite son! Of that she was certain. When God's grace heals our souls, He heals us so completely that sometimes we even forget the bad things that had happened. It was a foretaste of heaven.[21] There would be no more footprints of sorrow, at least, for a while.

Our self-chosen life script can be full of sound and fury, madness and the sins of idiots. Nevertheless, God's script for our life cannot be broken. If we sin, He chastens us and moves us back to the right track. If we learn faith *and* obedience, blessing and reward will follow.[22] God used that police officer on the Kansas interstate to pull me over, stop me dead in my tracks, spin me around and return me to His loving script already written for my life. Of course, at the time neither the police officer nor I was aware of this greater heavenly purpose; He was just doing his duty and I, my stupidity. But that is exactly my point. Of grace, I was unaware. Looking back, I am now convinced. Looking forward I know that His love and good script is inescapable. What the Lord did for me, He does for every baptized ordinary saint. You've got

---

21   "For behold, I create a new heavens and a new earth; and the former shall not be remembered or come to mind." Isaiah 65:17. Old memories erased by the Almighty and replaced by a greater and more powerful creation. Amazing.

22   "Many are the plans in the mind of a man, but it is the purpose of the Lord that will stand." Proverbs 19:21.

to believe this. It will bring you great peace of mind, if you do.

Search out your own evidence. See the invisible hand of God at work upon you. Understand His linkage. You can only bolter off the flight deck so many times in your life wasting precious years of your life, before God says, "Enough!" and then makes sure that your tailhook catches the arresting cable. Trapped by a loving God, you can go no further. He slams you back down onto the safe haven of His flight deck to be launched again according to His mission, not yours. His script is stronger than your script. And, guess what? It's tailored made just for you.

Barracuda Bust

"A Fire Hydrant, Seatbelts and Love"

Girls seemed to be a perpetual problem in my life. Looking back I clearly see that the whole athletic tough-guy persona thing was just

Luther High School South football team, 1967-68. Schreiber as half-back, number 42, bottom row, second from right. Note the tough-guy scowl!

camouflage to meet girls and secure a date. Most highschoolers act impulsively rarely thinking things through nor the consequences, short or long, of their actions and behaviors. That's precisely why they all need a loving God to watch over them every moment of the day. I was no exception, in fact, the boy who knew he would someday be a pastor, needed more watching than most.

Skipping a class while in high school was a brave, daring and Kool thing to do (not to mention dumb and stupid). If successful, it added a certain measure to the persona of a "tough-guy" bucking authority which then embellished your high school reputation and resumé.

One sunny afternoon during my senior year in late Spring, I snuck out of class during seventh-period study hour borrowing my buddy's car for a little joy ride. He had just purchased a 1964 used gold Plymouth Barracuda and tossed me the keys.

Two fellow classmates met me at the school door to the parking lot; a guy and a cute little sophomore blonde named Gretchen[23] who asked where I was going and if they could come along. I said yes little knowing that the course of my romantic life—despite all previous dead ends—would soon be greatly enhanced and dramatically altered for the next two years.

I was driving down 95th street going east approaching Western avenue when Gretchen asked if she could drive the car. Seeing I was anxious to get to know her better I said yes without asking if she had a driver's license and knew how to drive a car. She was 15. We pulled over on to a side street and exchanged positions with Gretchen taking the wheel. Her jolting start and stop at the corner of 95th street set off alarm bells immediately in my head. Before I could do anything she made a right turn on to 95th street, a four lane boulevard, and began to speed down the street.

"Do you know how to drive?" I asked her.

---

[23] The name of my former girlfriend has been changed in order to protect the guilty party, namely, me!

"Sure!" she replied. I remained nervous and unconvinced.

After weaving back and forth in the lane I yelled at her to make a right turn at the next corner on to a side street to exchange positions. She did . . . without braking. We swerved around the corner at about 30 miles per hour and were abruptly stopped by a fire hydrant which we hit dead center in the front of the grill bursting the radiator. Gretchen never hit the brakes. Impact speed? I guestimate about 25-30 miles per hour. The impact bounced my head off the windshield creating a circular outward bubble on the glass. My buddy who had been straddling the console bounced his head off the rear-view mirror and Gretchen banged her nose off the steering wheel and began to bleed. There is a moment after any car accident when your head spins and you don't know what happened or where you are. A quick assessment told me it could have been much worse. We all survived with only minor knicks and bruises.

In the 60's the Chicago cops were never very far away. A few moments later the police arrived, assessed the situation, gave me the ticket and had the car towed away. Strange way to meet a new girl but it worked and the new romance lasted for a couple of years into my sophomore year in college, at Northern Illinois University, Dekalb, Illinois.

"Where was that extraordinary grace of God this time?" you ask.

"Busy at work in our lives as usual," I reply.

If the impact speed had been slightly greater, I would have went through the windshield along with my buddy. Gretchen would easily have busted her nose and her rib cage on the steering wheel. The injuries to life and limb would have been severe most likely with scars for life flying through broken windshield glass. Oh, did I mention the fact that no one was wearing seatbelts? Seatbelts were just coming into vogue in those days. Most high school drivers thought they were extremely un-Kool and unnecessary so they were rarely worn and usually tucked back behind the seat and out of sight. Besides, how could your date snuggle up close to you while you were driving if you were both strapped down by a pair of seatbelts? Infallible logic to be sure yet quite stupid and dangerous, nonetheless. The grace of God still reigned over our stupidity and recklessness protecting us right through impact. God is good. His steadfast love never fails. You can count on it.

Hitchin' a Ride

"He makes His angels winds."
Hebrews 1:7

The new romance with Gretchen became a long distance relationship. I began my first semester at Northern Illinois University, Dekalb, Illinois, in January, 1969. Gretchen was finishing her senior year in high school in Lombard, Illinois. Hitchhiking was all the rage those days. Remember the band Vanity Fair and their hit smash single, "Hitchin' a Ride" released in 1969? By 1970 it went gold selling over a million copies in the USA. Every time my thumb went up, that real catchy tune filled my head and played my heart. There I stood on the berm of Illinois SR 38 just outside of Dekalb gesturing to every passing vehicle that I was ready to be picked up and transported to my girlfriend's home in Lombard.

Hitchhiking was the culture in the 60's. Hitchhiking could literally get you anywhere in the country if you could stand riding with strangers and offered a few bucks to the driver for gas. Most drivers would pick you up and drive reasonably safe. I know. I did it for the better part of a year any free weekend I had at college. I had no car in college, couldn't afford it. The distance from Dekalb to Lombard is about 50 miles, a one hour trip. Hitchhiking was my primary mode of transportation but it can be dangerous, extremely dangerous.

My thumb went up and a car stopped by. I jumped in headed for

HITCHIN' A RIDE

a romantic rendezvous in Lombard. I forget the make and model of the car but it was fast, big engine, lots of power and the driver wanted to show it off. He burned rubber leaving the berm and we tore down the highway cruising in excess of 80 miles per hour. Then he pushed the pedal to the metal. The speedometer needle leaped to 90, then 95, easily topping out at 100 miles per hour, without exaggeration. Remember, no seatbelts in those days, simply too un-Kool. When he went through a couple of intersections without stopping, I knew I had to get out of this car or my life would soon be scattered across some nearby cornfield. The good thing about hitchhiking is that the driver does not know exactly where you want to be dropped off. "Where are you headed?" can always elicit a vague response as you enter the car. After flying through a couple of intersections and passing cars on a two lane highway while accelerating uphill blindly approaching the summit, I knew it was time to bail out.

"Let me out at that gas station up ahead," I said. He obliged suspecting that I didn't appreciate his "race car" driving skills. He was right. He sped off in a cloud of dust and I was glad to be alive and standing on *terra firma*. At the moment, I didn't stop and thank God for being rescued but can you image the conversation of His holy angels who were flying beside the car at 100 miles per hour leaving a great turbulence of wind in their wake while protecting me?

"Hey Clyde, (angels do have names, you know), this kid is a real risk-taker! We're always doing double duty for him. My wings need a rest. I think it's time to ask the Boss for reassignment, if I can find a moment to spare!" Or so the conversation might have went.

Back down on earth, my next thought was simply, "Gotta find a safer driver next time. Off to Lombard!" Up went my thumb again bound for Lombard, and of His grace, vaguely aware.

Looking back, all I can say is that my attitude was reckless, dumb and stupid. I was ignorant of the perpetual, overshadowing, extraordinary grace of God surrounding my life, the life that He had personally redeemed through the cross of Christ. He was always keeping His covenant with me; I, on the other hand, had more important things in life to consider and pursue. In time, my ignorance would turn to thanksgiving but there were still a few more bolters and near crashes ahead before landing safely on the flight deck of God's celestial grace.

Lights Out

"The ruins of time build mansions in eternity."
William Blake[24]

The romance that began with a car crash now ended with a bang. One Friday night late in the Fall semester of 1970, after hitchin' a ride from Dekalb to Lombard and walking a few blocks to Gretchen's house, I knocked on the door expecting to see her pretty face greet me. Instead, it was the face of her mother who told me that Gretchen was out and would not be home until later that evening. Well, I accepted the news in the good spirit in which it was given but suspected something was wrong seeing Gretchen knew I was coming in that Friday evening. Hitchin' a ride does not run like a bus schedule. Sometimes I was lucky and would get in early on a Friday night but at other times, quite late. So, if she stepped out to do a little errand or something at the last minute, I understood and I could wait.

And wait I did. 9 o'clock, 10 o'clock, 11 o'clock, Midnight. Still no Gretchen. Her mother was short on details even after my prying questions and seemed unconcerned about her safety. She went to bed. So, I concluded, for whatever reason, Gretchen must be out on a date with someone else. I sprawled out on the couch, wide awake in a dark living room, staring at the ceiling, nerves frazzled and anger boiling up

---

24 Geoffrey Keyes Kt., ed. *The Letters of William Blake* (Great Britain: Oxford University Press, 1980). Blake was an English poet, 1757-1827. (Public Domain).

inside me. All I could do now was wait for the sound of a car to pull up in the driveway.

Around 2 AM a car's headlights beamed through the front picture window, flooding the living room with light and black shadows that slowly moved across the wall. I leaped from the couch, grabbed my brown leather jacket—it was almost winter outside—open and slammed the front door shut and walked quickly to the car. There behind the wheel was someone I did not know from Adam sitting next to my girl holding what appeared to be a rather intense conversation. He saw me glaring at him through the window and much to my surprise he rolled down the window and asked, "Can I help you?" That was his first mistake.

I stared through the open car window, trying to make out in the dark who I was dealing with as he started to open the door. That was his second mistake. I responded by yanking the door out of his hand pulling it all the way open. I dragged him out of the car and then slammed him against the side of the car.

"Who do you think you are dating my girl?" I screamed at him. Whatever he said next, I forget. It didn't matter. My anger was a fiery rage, exploding, and my fist was raised and cocked to punch his lights out. Nothing was going to stop me.

At that moment, Gretchen came racing around the back of the car shouting, "Don't hit him! Don't hit him!" and tried to calm me down. I slammed him again into the car and then walked away. In the midst of this raging emotion, surprisingly, I had one logical unemotional thought. Gretchen must have been the one who initiated the date not him. She's the problem, not him.

The next morning we had a talk. It wasn't very long nor very substantive. The content is a bit foggy, but I do remember her saying, "I don't want to be a pastor's wife." So that's what this is all about? Looking back now it all seems understandable. But at that point in time, it hurt and it hurt bad. Gretchen was not pastor wife material, and for the record, neither was I pastor material. Nevertheless, the gifts and calling of God are irrevocable. Romans 11:29.[25] The little boy who had once said to Grandma, "I'm going to be a pastor!" could not escape the strong emotion that his vocation was sealed for life and still open to pursue regardless of the present circumstances.

Where was God's extraordinary grace when my competition drove up the driveway at 2 a.m.? Did God even care? Was He on vacation in some distant galaxy fixing somebody else's problem? I had no idea our romance was in danger, let alone that it would end that way. The whole affair had blindsided me but God's extraordinary grace intervened precisely at the moment when I was ready to slam my cocked fist into his face. I was so angry that one punch would not have satisfied me until I would have knocked him to the ground. Who knows how badly I might have hurt him? I felt incredibly strong at that moment filled with a dark rage. It was a fight I wasn't going to lose but God stopped me before the first punch was thrown. Just like He stopped Abraham of old from plunging the knife into his son's chest before offering him as a sacrifice to God, so too God stopped me, at just the right time. His timing is always perfect. His extraordinary grace reigned supreme at a very dark moment in my life, my ordinary life.

God spun me around that night. He pointed me in a new direction. In time He healed my broken heart and ruined love life, ruins that would be transformed and rewritten by His gracious script. He said, "Now I'm going to begin to make a pastor out of you." The days of proving to myself and others what a tough guy I thought I was had come to an end. Thank God. A new mission in life would soon be launched off the flight deck of God's celestial grace for He had just recovered me from crashing into the angry sea.

---

25   "Irrevocable," as in without regret, not to be repented of, nor to be changed from the original decision made. God's grace upon you is life-long, unchangeable and greater than any sin or any personal history of sinning.

PART TWO:
Grace Manifested

Searching for Truth

"Dunkin' Donuts"

You might conclude from the episodes described in Part I above; namely, the tough guy persona and reckless behavior that I was an academic drop-out, quite the contrary. Lutherans pride themselves on an excellent education. It is foundational to being a solid Lutheran Christian. Kids should be smart, disciplined and respect their elders.

For over one hundred years, St. Andrew Lutheran grade school excelled in offering a strong traditional curriculum.[26] Both my mother and I went to the same grade school in Chicago (during different years, of course!) During my school years, all the teachers from first grade through eighth grade were male, German, strict and disciplined. My report cards were filled with a lot of A's, a moderate amount of B's and rarely a C.

Following grade school, by the second year at Luther High School South, I and six other students were selected for the Advanced Latin class where we did our work separately from the main class in the library. The "fun" began in my junior and senior year of High School and ran through college when my priorities were sports, girls and partying—not necessarily in that order. Yet, the inescapable voice in the back of my head and in my heart through all those years remained immovable regarding the pastoral vocation. No matter what my peers may have thought of me at the time, my vocational destiny was sealed, a pastor I would be. There was no other real competition.[27]

---

26 My eight grade report card listed the following subjects taught every day and a few weekly at St. Andrew; Religion, memorization, church history, reading, language, spelling, geography, history, citizenship, arithmetic, health, general science, music, art, handwriting and physical education. This was the standard list of subjects taught with few variations from 1st thru 8th grade in the 1950s.

27 Well, I guess I should mention one other short-lived competition. For a while, I wanted to be a jet fighter pilot somewhere around the 4th grade but that destiny was squelched by poor eyesight. I wore glasses from Kindergarten through 4th grade with a half patch over one eye in

Infant baptism, as the church has practiced it for centuries, requires the suspension of a certain amount of reason, some would say all reason. It seems reasonable that a person should be baptized at his or her own request, when they are ready to make their own sincere decisions in life about important matters. Wouldn't you agree? It also seems reasonable that until a child has grown up mentally and understands the words and the meaning of baptism, it would be meaningless to foist upon the innocent infant child the sacrament of baptism which they cannot recall nor remember later in life. Wouldn't you also agree? And besides, if every person under the sun has free will in earthly and spiritual matters, as is reasonably assumed by most adults, why mess with it? Why not just let the individual come to church, come to Christ and come to God whenever they finally get around to it? Wouldn't you most heartedly agree?!

Such thoughts filled my head my senior year in college as seminary loomed next on the horizon. I had a multitude of theological discussions on the subject with campus pastor Rev. E. George Krause[28] in his office followed by multiple hours spent in the church's library reading the theological commentaries of great lights in church history on the subject. After all my research, however, I still remained unconvinced that infant baptism was a God-pleasing thing. It was time to take matters into one's own hands and push God for a clear cut answer on the

---

my early years because of lazy eye syndrome. For a while my grade school buddies called me "four eyes." You need 20/20 vision to fly a fighter jet and to be able to see what you're shooting at. Uncle Sam preferred two good eyes, not four. Becoming a jet jockey fighter pilot was not in the footprints of God.

28 Rev. E. George Krause was the campus pastor at Immanuel Lutheran Church adjacent to Northern Illinois University during the years of my attendance (1969-1973) in Dekalb, Illinois. His sermons were always relevant and enlightening. He counseled me on a broad array of my personal concerns as well as theological topics. No matter how busy he would be, if anyone needed to speak with him, he would rise from his desk, sit in a chair next to you and give you his full attention. More than once, I joined him on pastoral visits to his parishioners in nursing homes. To me he was always a bright light shining in a dark place and I welcomed his good counsel on every occasion. He served as pastor at Immanuel from 1960 until his death in 2010 at the age of 84. He loved literature, especially Shakespeare and languages. He loved people and was an astute observer and interpreter of God's wonderful creation. Pastor Krause was well loved and beloved by his congregation.

subject. I demanded an answer!

Pentecostalism was on the rise on the NIU campus and in American culture in the late 60's and early 70's. Pentecostalism rejected infant baptism and taught that it should be replaced by full immersion water baptism with the resultant conclusive evidence of speaking in tongues as firm proof that you were now filled with the Holy Spirit. If one is to do the work of God as a pastor, how much better could it be done if one is filled with the Spirit! So I reasoned. If my infant baptism was displeasing to God it is no wonder that I am not experiencing the full power of His Spirit. If I were re-baptized—so I convinced myself—then I would most certainly emerge from the dunking tank full of the Spirit and explosive joy speaking in a heavenly language known only to God Himself. I was convinced I had solved the theological dilemma and had discovered the next footprint of God for my life.

Late in the Spring semester of my senior year at college, I was re-baptized at a non-denominational Christian church in Dekalb. When the big moment arrived, I donned a white baptismal robe and proceeded to the baptismal tank. "In the name of the Father, and of the Son and of the Holy Spirit, I baptize you. . ." spoke the pastor. I went under for the third time in the name of the Triune God, now completely soaked, fully expecting to burst forth in uncontrollable joy and ecstatic utterances as my face surfaced from the baptismal tank. Nothing happened. Nothing, not even a small gurgling syllable. As I wiped the water from my eyes all I could see and hear was the applause of the witnesses around me but my tongue remained silent, uninspired and immovable in my mouth. No joy. No ecstasy. No spontaneous speaking in tongues. No overwhelming dousing by the Holy Spirit. Just wet all over.

What had gone wrong? Had I not obeyed the Word of God? Had He not led me to this moment? Is God a liar? Does His Word offer false, empty and vain promises? What was the problem? All that research, all those prayers, all that seeking. What a bummer. God was a big disappointment. Little did I know at the time, I was reading the wrong script, again.

The passage of time on any important life-event often admits perspective and hopefully, a little wisdom. How many times do you have to "dunk the donut" for efficacy? Maybe, just maybe, it wasn't God's fault. Perhaps my faith wasn't strong enough, or trusting enough or fervent enough to receive His promise. Perhaps my theology was all screwed up. I was confused and more than a little let down. The "You're only half-a-Christian" theology that my charismatic friends had pumped into my head in college "until you receive the fullness of the Spirit and speak in tongues" was now at stake in my mind and losing ground. I hadn't fully rejected infant baptism but I hadn't fully accepted adult immersion baptism either.[29] You might say I was suspended between a cup and a bucket of water. How much water anyway does it take to produce a legitimate baptism and bring down the Holy Spirit? One dunk? Two dunks?? Three dunks??? Dunkin' donut questions are guaranteed to beget dunkin' donut wrong answers.

Baptism begins the script of God in your life which protects you against reckless theological misinterpretation of His Word, as I would soon learn. With an open mind and willing to be convinced of the truth from God's Word, I launched into a new mission and matriculated at Concordia Theological Seminary, Springfield, Illinois, in the summer of 1973. But first, another theological disappointment from God loomed on the near horizon.

---

29 In the case of infant baptism, where there is no personal recollection of the day you were baptized, you trust the word of your parents, a Baptismal certificate and the church records. If you are old enough to remember your Baptism, good for you, however, in either case regardless of age rarely do I hear any Christian bring up the subject of Baptism in daily conversation as the source and center of his/her strength, courage and trust in Christ in order to renounce sin and survive the days of pain and sorrow. After all the strident historical and hysterical hullabaloo over the mode of Baptism, the essential meaning of Baptism has been largely forgotten and rarely preached, namely, that the old man has been buried and crucified with Christ and the new man has been birthed by the waters of baptism united to the resurrection of Christ. How can you live out and believe the script of God without constant reference to your baptism in Christ Jesus? How can you learn to turn from sin in any temptation and live for God without the anchor of Baptism as the new reality for your soul? Simple answer . . . you can't.

Forsake All!

> *"There is meaning in every journey that is unknown to the traveler."*
> *Dietrich Bonhoeffer.*[30]

After the failure to receive the full measure of the Spirit through rebaptism, I went back to the Scriptures searching for where I went wrong.[31] All of the discipleship passages in the Gospels[32] seemed to leap off the page and convict me that I still was not totally dedicated to the Savior and His mission. I was not at His disposal 24/7 and ready to obey His voice. Ridicule from others was not the problem. Whatever ridicule I anticipated from such obedience to the Savior didn't bother me. The next step forward seemed to be a literal forsaking of all that I owned. After which, I would simply rely one hundred percent upon the Lord to provide everything I need and to lead me, daily.

Most, if not all, commentators describe the discipleship passages as "Gospel imperatives" meaning that obedience to such does not save the soul but rather describes the goal and ideal of the Christian life, that is, to put Christ Jesus first in the heart, mind and soul in all things. That's easier said than done. In fact, I reasoned that it would be easier just to get up and literally forsake all, wait on God, and trust Him that the next voice I hear would be His to guide me throughout the day, as opposed to actually trying to keep Christ first in all my thoughts and

---

30 https://bibleportal.com/bible-quote/there-is-meaning-in-every-journey-that-is-unknown-to-the-traveler. Dietrich Bonhoeffer. (accessed May, 2023)

31 The year after college and before matriculation into the seminary (1973) was spent comfortably at my parent's home in Springfield, Missouri, which would be their new residence for the next 35 years. The south side of Chicago was now permanently in the rearview mirror for the family. I spent the year doing a number of odd jobs from driving an orange juice/dairy truck to a waiter at Hickory Hills country club in order to save money for the seminary.

32 Luke 14:26, 33. "If anyone comes to Me and does not hate his father and mother, wife and children, brothers and sisters, yes, and his own life also, he cannot be My disciple. . . whoever of you does not forsake all that he has cannot be My disciple." The cost of discipleship is unequivocal. It will cost you your life. See similar passages: Mt. 10:37-39; Mark 8:34-38.

FORSAKE ALL!

behavior during the day which seemed to be an impossible task. Why not live your life just like the first disciples who walked with the Lord and simply followed Him wherever He went? If Jesus talked directly to them, why wouldn't He talk directly with me too? So, I decided it was time to forsake all; house, home, Mom, Dad, and my brothers. Time to set out on my own obeying the Lord for *terra incognita*.[33]

The first problem was to decide what to take with me. To forsake all literally means to leave everything behind, so I reasoned. Do I own the shirt on my back, the pants on my legs, the shoes on my feet? If I did they too should be left behind. Does that mean that I should walk down the street naked waiting for the next voice from God? Now that's a pretty risqué picture not to mention what the neighbors might think! Piercing the perplexity of my own troubled thoughts came a shot of relief. The very clothes I am wearing were recently bought by Mom, therefore, it is not necessary to forsake them and disrobe in order to fulfill the Lord's command because they really don't belong to me anyway. My clothes were a gift. It was small relief but at least I would not have to walk out of the house stitch-stark naked down the street in front of the neighbors.

Time of day? About 11 a.m. Mom was in the kitchen. I had been reading the Bible all morning (as usual). I exited my bedroom and said, "I'm going to take a walk." Mom nodded in agreement, mumbled something, and that was that.

Once out the door, I turned right and began walking up the street from the folk's home on Woodland avenue, Springfield, Missouri. With every step I took I kept looking heavenward, waiting for the voice of God. One block, still waiting. Two blocks, still waiting. Three blocks, waiting still. At the end of the street was a prairie where I stopped and prayed to God fervently and waited, and waited, and waited. No response. No emotional touch. No whisper from God, just silence, deafening, disappointing, empty silence. If God is for real and He wants

---

33   Land unknown, territory unexplored.

me to serve Him, then where the heck is He? Why does He hide from me? I'm ready to do great things for Him. What went wrong this time?

I turned around, walked back down the street and in the front door about two hours later. "How was your walk?" Mom said, "Where did you go?"

"Oh, it was alright . . . just down the street," I mumbled. And that was that but the guilt from not actually waiting a bit longer for the voice of God condemned me for years to come. Should I have waited another hour? Another two hours? Perhaps all night? The fault was still all mine, so I believed. "Forsake all and follow Me!" remained an unfulfilled command, something I didn't do literally or completely. If it is perfect obedience that God wants, even just perfect practical obedience, I screwed up again. God was justified in not blessing me fully. It was just another bolter off the flight deck into the angry turbulent sea of life.

Return to Lincoln Land

"The beginning of wisdom starts with NT Greek grammar."[34]

It was time to go back to school. Orientation at Concordia Theological Seminary, Springfield, Illinois, 1973, was scheduled for July of that summer. In the small group sessions, I voiced my concern that I would remain open minded about the many theological issues of the day, study the Scriptures honestly and search for the truth religiously. I was greatly complimented for my "open-mindedness" by a faculty member. Apparently, it was a very rare event to hear such an attitude in

---

34 Dr. Buls, Professor of Greek, Concordia Seminary, Springfield, Illinois, Winter quarter, Gospel of Luke, 1973-74. Of course, this is not an exact quote but it expresses the reverence and spirit of his exegetical love for the sacred text in the original languages which he sought to impart and inculcate upon his students in every class he taught.

the history of theological conversations at the seminary.

Traditional conservative seminaries across denominations usually have four-themed areas of concentration or departments; namely, historical, systematic, exegetical and practical departments. The student will pick his concentration early during the course of his graduate studies and complete the sufficient number of courses required for graduation. My thinking from the outset was to choose the exegetical department and to focus on the original languages of Scripture.

Historical theology opens up the long perspective of doctrinal debate throughout church history. Systematic theology ties together into a supportive whole all the major doctrines of Scripture. The practical department places the emphasis on teaching and preaching but the exegetical department dives deep in the original languages of Scripture seeking the intended sense. That's for me. I figured if I knew for certain the intended sense of God's Word from the original tongues then preaching, teaching and illustrating His truth would be monumentally easier than just trying to ascertain meaning from a variety of English translations. After all, the doctrine of verbal inspiration ascribes Divine inspiration to the very words and grammar of Scripture, that is, Greek and Hebrew, in the original tongues, not to subsequent translations in other languages which can reflect the truth accurately but sometimes miss the mark and the nuances of the original script.

The "meatball" was now in sight. I "called the ball" as God's guiding lights on the horizon brought me safely in. The glide slope to the flight deck of His sacred languages was right on target. I was trapped by the arresting cable of His good grace that triggered a shower of exegetical sparks in my heart and mind.

Ambition to Excel

> Ignorance is the beginning of wisdom.[35]

I thought I knew the Bible well before I entered the seminary. After all, being raised in the Lutheran educational system for 12 years meant a heavy dose of religion inculcated upon every young, inquiring and growing mind. The Lutheran system provides an ample supply of prooftexts one could ever need to support any doctrine from the Bible. But Scripture proof-texts, to be effective in defending the faith, must be memorized and internalized. Of course, rote memorization with or without understanding was always necessary to pass any religion class. This was the Lutheran road to prepare the young soul to receive the Lord's Supper by 8th the grade through the Rite of Confirmation.

Sitting at the feet of seminary professors well versed in Greek and Hebrew presents a real dilemma for the average seminarian upon matriculation. In first year of seminary I was sure that whatever my profs were trying to teach me, I already knew being an avid student of the King James Bible. By the end of the second year of seminary, I began to realize that perhaps, maybe, just maybe, they might know some doctrines of Scripture better than me. At least their systematic compilation of various passages in support of doctrine, life and guidance for all *pastor-wanna-bees* seemed a bit more cogent than my current mental theological stew and state of mind. By the end of the fourth year of seminary, I was convinced that I knew very little of Scripture rightly, nor had I harmonized it properly, and my hermeneutics were hardly Christ-centered. Therefore I reluctantly conceded that my profs were probably godly men, solidly educated and far more well-versed in Greek and Hebrew than I was.

---

35 Ignorance can be the beginning of wisdom in so far as one recognizes the limitations of his/her own mind and turns to the Creator for true understanding. "Get wisdom! Get understanding! Do not forget nor turn away from the words of my mouth. Do not forsake her and she will preserve you; love her, and she will keep you." Proverbs 4:5, 6.

Maybe, just maybe, I had to admit, they might know the Bible a little bit better than I did. It was a humble if not an arrogant confession. I had been fouled momentarily on the flight deck, caught in the emergency rigging of God's restraining good grace.

Holy Toledo!

For all the saints who from their labors rest,
Who Thee by faith before the world confessed.
Thy name, O Jesus, be forever blest.
Alleluia! Alleluia![36]

The third year of the seminary's four year graduate curriculum is the vicarage year. Toward the end of the second year, a vicarage call service in held in the Spring. Every *pastor-wannabe* receives a call to serve one year in an LCMS congregation under the spiritual tutelage of the congregation's pastor. During the assignment/call service the candidate's name is called out and the church where he will serve. Surprises and excitement abound because no one knows where they are going until that moment in the call service. My family including my older brother Neil was present for the call service. When my assignment was called out, Neil, in his typical extroverted, exuberant Marine Corps voice shouted out, "Holy Toledo!" He was right on two counts. My vicarage would be a holy and inspirational ministry under the guidance of Pastor O. H. Bertram, and there I would meet, greet and fall in love with Connie Cramer, the love of my earthly life, whom I would wed in holy matrimony on June 19, 1977 at Good Shepherd Lutheran Church, "Holy" Toledo, Ohio, Pastor Bertram officiating. So much for the monk's life of study, meditation and solitary confinement!

---

36   *The Lutheran Hymnal.* (St. Louis, Missouri: Corcordia Publishing House, 1941). #463. "For All the Saints Who From Their Labors Rest." (Public Domain).

Unlike the attempted first kiss years earlier on Sharon's front porch, my first kiss with Connie on her front porch sealed the deal. I could resist no longer. The monk's life was in my rearview mirror receding forever. Thank God! It was His footprint and His script and the script turned out so much better than I could have ever dreamed.

Vicarage under Pastor Bertram was a marvelous adventure. Within the span of about 10 years Pastor Bertram had taken his congregation from a flock of less than 50 souls to a congregation pushing 1,000 souls by the time I arrived (1975/76). He shaped many of my thoughts on evangelism and outreach to this very day. He always said that a good Pastor should wear out the soles of his shoes taking care of the souls of his flock while reaching out to the souls in his community. He practiced what he preached. Pastor Bertram began the TV program called, "Worship for Shut-Ins," [37] a half-hour worship program broadcasted on 10 plus TV stations around the country at that time. He also wrote a regular column for the local Toledo Blade newspaper that was syndicated and printed in other newspapers. Weekly, Pastor Bertram appeared on local Toledo TV with a five minute segment entitled, "Religion in the News." Everywhere Pastor Bertram went in Toledo he wore his clerical collar. He was well known in the community and wanted to be well-known for the Gospel's sake. Whenever I would go out with him for a mid-morning coffee break at a local restaurant, half the guests in the restaurant would come to his table, nod and greet him by name.

Not too long after I arrived, Pastor Bertram sent me out to make cold calls in a nearby trailer park one hot summer day. No better way to practice evangelism than to dive in, knock on doors and introduce yourself, he said. An elderly, petite slightly frail woman answered the door and after my brief introduction decided it was safe to let me in for a conversation about God and the church. Half way through my Gospel presentation, someone else knocked on the door. It was two Jehovah's

---

37   "Worship for Shut-Ins" continues to this day housed and broadcasted from the campus of Concordia Theological Seminary, Fort Wayne, Indiana served by a variety of guest preachers.

Witnesses who happen to be canvassing the same trailer park. The elderly woman with the pleasant demeanor also invited them to "join" our conversation. So, there we were, the three of us; the fresh-out-of-the-box vicar and two JWs sitting next to me trying to hold a three-way conversation with the woman. The more they talked and the more I talked the more the woman became confused especially when the JWs began touting their "knowledge" of the Greek NT to try and prove that Jesus was not the Son of God but just a son of God, to whom we should all aspire and emulate for our salvation. I knew they didn't know Greek nor we're they actually Christian because they assert that Christ Jesus is not the Savior of the world but merely a fine example to follow on the pathway to your salvation so I proposed a deal. I said, "Let's meet again here next week at this woman's trailer and this time you bring your head-elder or whoever is knowledgeable in NT Greek and we'll discuss together the first chapter of the Gospel of John. I said, "Let the woman decide who is telling the truth. Fair enough?" Surprisingly they agreed.

The following week we all met and sat together in the woman's trailer; the head-elder from JW, his assistant and me. Remember the old adage? "A little knowledge is a dangerous thing," and again, "False knowledge is even more dangerous than ignorance." The conversation did not go well with the JWs toward the woman. The head JW elder was easily refuted by Scripture and my knowledge of NT Greek. The woman saw and understood the difference and within a week she was baptized by water in the name of the Triune God

The new vicar giving the senior pastor a lesson in churchmanship.

at Good Shepherd Lutheran Church by Pastor Bertram. Some day we will get much better acquainted in heaven. God's saving footprints had arrived just in time in her life.

Pastor Bertram frequently said to me during my vicarage year that he loved the ministry and hoped and prayed the Lord would give him a long and prosperous earthly ministry. Three years after my vicarage, 1979, I received the sad news that Pastor Bertram had passed away from pancreatic cancer. He was only 61. The Lord's script for his life didn't quite match his servant's expectations but to depart this life and be with the Lord is a far better thing. (Philippians 1:23) The script of Pastor Bertram's life was now complete. The last leaf had fallen from the tree of his life. He, the faithful saint of God, had now been catapulted off the bow of the flight deck into the arms of the Everlasting Father, the Prince of Peace. He remains to this day a very blessed memory to all who knew and loved him.

A Lot of Learning is a Good Thing!

"Purkel" mimeograph ink, sharpened pencils and pink erasers.[38]

Does romantic love mean that I have to give up my studies or intellectual pursuits? One can kiss and read books at the same time, wouldn't you agree? Well almost. My thirst for knowledge greatly increased after

---

38 I distinctly remember the intoxicating smell of the "purkel" (as my four year old granddaughter, Natalie, loves to say) mimeograph ink they used at St. Andrew Lutheran grade school. The pleasant aroma served as a kind of intellectual aphrodisiac to lure reluctant students into their books. It worked for me! I was hooked. I enjoyed the endless trips made to the pencil sharpener hanging on the wall by the cloak-room door. The pencil could never be sharp enough. My desk interior for books, papers, pencils and pink erasers was always neatly organized. The sound of the teacher's white chalk gliding across 4 x 12 foot blackboards, the frenetic arm shuffle of the "eraser-volunteers" cleaning the blackboards at the end of the school day, all bring back pleasant memories. The smell of autumn leaves burning in the breeze often drifted through the school room windows on bright beautiful Fall days imprinting only one thought on my mind, "It's time for school and new adventures in learning!"

I returned to the seminary which now had been transplanted to Fort Wayne, Indiana[39] where I finished my 4th year graduating May, 1977.

Most of the students at the seminary say that there are two great hurdles to becoming a Pastor in the LCMS; the first, learning NT Greek which must be acquired in the summer before matriculation and before taking any classes in the regular curriculum (if the student is deficient in this area), and the second, passing WAM's Romans class[40] which was usually taken in the second year of seminary. The difficulty with Professor Walter A. Maier's class was that his verbal delivery was similar to an uninterrupted volley of words burped out of a machine-gun. He expected you to take notes furiously, remember almost everything he said and then discharge the details down on to the blank pages of a blue test booklet in logical order. He was known for not passing some students. His class was mandatory for all students. No detours around this one.

In the 70's mini-cassette tape recorders were in vogue. I figured if I was going to pass his class I needed to tape his lectures, transcript them word-for-word and memorize all the material for his test. This I did religiously and it paid off handsomely. I aced every exam and passed his Romans class. I also developed quite a fondness for the man, his knowledge of Scripture and the enlightenment my soul and spirit received under his teaching. WAM became my MDiv thesis advisor. By the time I finished my 4th year of seminary I had taken five exegetical courses with Dr. Maier, aced them all and graduated with 21 hours of coursework more than was needed for graduation.

39　The distance from Toledo, Ohio to Springfield, Illinois is over 400 miles and 6 hours by car. The distance between Toledo and Fort Wayne, Indiana is only 100 miles and less than two hours by car. Thus, it appears to me highly plausible that God moved the entire seminary in my last year of studies just so I could visit Connie more frequently and keep the romance alive until we wedded, June 19th, 1977, one month after graduation. What a gracious felicitous footprint of God! Well, okay, maybe's it's a wee bit of a stretch, nevertheless, it worked out wonderfully.

40　Dr. Walter A. Maier, Jr. affectionately called "WAM" by his students deserved the sobriquet due to his rapid machine-gun style of lecturing. His father, Dr. Walter Maier, Sr. was a PhD Harvard graduate in Old Testament semitic studies and the founder and first nationally known speaker of The Lutheran Hour. I greatly admired both father and son. Dr. Maier Sr. was my inspiration to originally pursue graduate studies in Old Testament and Hebrew.

Almost everywhere I served either as a parish pastor (Pittsburgh, PA, Jacksonville, FL, Lake City, FL) or on active duty (Jacksonville, NC, Norfolk, VA, New Orleans, LA) I was either taking classes at the local university, or teaching a course in religion, or teaching Biblical Hebrew or Greek at a community college. Where did this grand romance for all things academic begin? I'm guessing at St. Andrew Lutheran grade school.

I love school! Learning is such a good thing! And God's script for my life was replete with a wide diversity of learning and teaching opportunities from teaching regular church adult bible classes in church to High School German in the public school to Doctoral level classes for military chaplains. It was a script I could never have written out for myself. All I had to do was to place my feet squarely in His steps before me and walk by faith and faith alone.[41]

Bethel Lutheran Church
Glenshaw, Pennsylvania

"You're in Steeler Country now."[42]

My first call to serve as the pastor in my own church was to Steeler country, Bethel Lutheran church in Glenshaw, a suburb of Pittsburgh, PA, 1977-1982. It was a rock solid conservative orthodox Lutheran congregation and a great place to cut your theological teeth in the ministry, plant roots and raise a family. Bethel worshipped about 100 souls on a Sunday and despite all the cold calls in the neighborhood and evangelism workshops, when I left for my first tour of active duty five

---

41 "Delight yourself in the Lord and He will give you the desires of your heart." Psalm 37:4
42 Spoken by Fred Harmon, a faithful member and pillar of Bethel Lutheran Church, one Sunday morning to his new pastor. Fred was intending to indoctrinate Connie and I into the milieu of the new culture we had just entered. It almost worked!

BETHEL LUTHERAN CHURCH GLENSHAW, PENNSYLVANIA

SATURDAY-SUNDAY, AUG. 6-7, 1977 — NEWS RECORD—11

BETHEL'S MINISTER — The Rev. Mark and Connie Schreiber, standing on the steps of Bethel Lutheran Church, Scott Avenue, Shaler. The Rev. Mr. Schreiber was installed as pastor of the church July 10.

North Hills News Record

years later in 1982, Bethel was still worshipping about 100 souls per Sunday. However, the Lord always rewards the labor done in His name, if not in this life then in the life to come. He alone maintains the number of the saved in His congregations, nevertheless, it was an exciting first five years living out the script God had written for me.

Our first daughter, Amanda Mary, was born in Pittsburgh, August 23, 1979. She was the baby darling of the congregation. Every Sunday she was passed around, held and cradled by our affectionate saints at Bethel. One of the elders, Elmer Mauerhoff, used to cradle Mandy in his arms walking up and down the basement of the church while singing an old hit tune from Irving Berlin's White Christmas:

> Mandy, there's a minister handy
> And it sure would be dandy, if we'd let him make a fee.
> So don't you linger, here's the ring for your finger
> Isn't it a humdinger?
> Come along and let the wedding chimes, bring happy times
> For Mandy and me.[43]

The Pittsburgh Steelers were team of the decade in 70s. They won back-to-back Super Bowls in 1974 and 75 and again in 1978 and 79. Of course, I was a loyal Chicago Bears fan and could care less about the Steelers no matter how rabid some of the younger members at Bethel might be about their home team. So, as a test of loyalty to the true Lutheran orthodox faith, I scheduled a church congregational meeting for Super Bowl Sunday XIV, January 20, 1980. I laid down the law stating that anyone excusing themselves from participation in the congregational meeting in lieu of watching the Super Bowl would be putting their spiritual lives in danger by placing worldly things above church business. I was only two years and a half years into the ministry,

---

43   From Irving Berlin's *White Christmas*, released Jan. 1, 1954. Mandy is sung by the crooner, Bing Crosby. Lyrics published before January 1, 1928 and in the Public Domain. https://en.wikisource.org/wiki/Mandy.

but I sure was ready to show them who was in charge and that I really meant business! Mercifully, in a face-saving gesture (my face, that is) one of the Elders suggested we move the church meeting to early Sunday afternoon thereby leaving the members enough time—assuming the church meeting didn't last too long—to return home and watch the game, if they liked. It was a swell face-saving compromise followed by one of the shortest congregational meetings on record. The Steelers won handily that Sunday, defeating the LA Rams, 31-19 with QB Terry Bradshaw at the helm. I hate to think now what the good saints would have done to me that Sunday if the Steelers had lost. Sometimes it is not an issue of stepping in God's footprints, it's just a matter of stepping "in it!"

The five years spent as Pastor of Bethel Lutheran Church were good years, formative years supported by wonderful, strong, solid Lutheran Christians. The church came with a parsonage which was a Godsend for Connie and me. All we needed to do was to supply the house with furniture and love. There was no shortage of love, buying furniture would take some time.

The street in front of the parsonage on Arden drive sloped downhill and east toward Mount Royal cemetery a mere 50 yards or less at the end of the street. One would think that strolling through a cemetery during your first years in the ministry would be a morbid thing, but Connie and I discovered it was a great place to collect one's thoughts. I often preached to the dead while walking up and down the pathways of the cemetery. The dead never once broke their silence and interrupted my eloquent sermonettes and, of course, neither did they applaud.

Before we arrived, the parsonage had been vacant for at least six months. When we moved into the parsonage around the 4th of July, 1977, some nocturnal visitors had already preceded us. True to graveyard legend and lore, most cemeteries had a fair number of bats hanging around. Every evening the sky over Arden drive would fill with bats swirling low to the ground darting left and right sucking up insects with their radar hearing. Unknown to us, the bats had been able to slither into the house between the slats at the top of the A-frame roof. Once inside, they made themselves comfortable inside the walls of the parsonage.

The very first morning after moving in, I went downstairs to the unfinished basement in order to check out the garage door which was manually operated. As I walked past the stationary tub I looked inside and noticed what I thought was a frog resting peacefully in the bottom of the tub. Upon closer inspection—not being a professional rodent examiner—something told me intuitively that this lowly creature was not a frog. Nope, it was a bat. It looked quite dead but when I poked it with a stick it became quite alive. Bats are creepy, slimy and disgusting creatures. Hard to believe they are part of God's creation but nevertheless, I had no intention of sharing my house with a bunch of slimy bats. The immediate question was how to kill this one before it could get away and call in reinforcements. I looked around the basement and not too far away from the tub was a bucket. Ideal, I thought! I would annihilate the bat by asphyxiation if I could just get the bucket on top of the bat. In one quick anxious and surreptitious move, I slammed the bucket down over the bat which immediately interrupted its bat dreams. It sprang to life and tried frantically to get out from under the bucket. The bat's energy to escape convinced me quickly that suffocation would take longer than I would care to wait. Since it was in the stationary tub inside a bucket, the brilliant idea popped into the mind that I could drown him to death. All I have to do is turn on the spigot, and so I did. It didn't occur to me that the rising water in the tub would begin to push the bucket up unless I stood there holding the bucket down. Now the bat was greatly agitated and more furious than ever flopping around inside a confined space, breathing and surviving in the small pocket of air the upside-down bucket had now created. Now what to do? If I left the stationary tub the bucket would flip over and the bat would buzz around the basement. Nowhere nearby or in sight was a heavy object that I could place on top of the bucket to keep the bat trapped. I had no idea how long the bat could survive under such conditions nor did I want to hang around and find out.

Beside the stationary tub within reach were two bottles; one was bleach, the other ammonia. I grabbed the bleach bottle. If this didn't kill him, at least I would have the cleanest albino bat in Pittsburgh. I poured in bleach sufficient enough to kill a dozen bats. Three minutes later, the bat had not slowed down one wit; it was still furiously pounding the sides of the bucket with its wings. Perhaps, if I added a little ammonia to the bleach water, the toxic chemicals would surely do him in. With a sinister smirk, I poured in a generous amount of ammonia. What happened next is covered with brain fog. Apparently, bleach mixed with ammonia can produce quite a toxic cloud to the nostrils. I took one whiff of my poisonous concoction, recoiled instantly from the tub and almost knocked myself out. The mixture created an overwhelming pungent odor that no creature could breathe and live long. As I recoiled from the tub, I was sure the bucket would tip over and the bat would escape but within a few seconds after the poisonous cloud dispersed throughout the basement, I crept quietly back to the tub to investigate. No sounds were heard. No whirring of wings. No flip-flops within the bucket. Slowly, I lifted the bucket. The water spooled quietly out of the tub. There lying motionless on the bottom of the tub was one dead bat. Exhilaration! Joy! Happiness secured. Mission accomplished. I would sleep well that night knowing that I, the self-appointed batman of the church, had made the parsonage safe from all flying intruders. The Bethel Lutheran bat caper had been brought to permanent closure.[44]

---

[44] Little did I anticipate at the time that within three years the bats would return. Here's the scenario. I had just returned on a Sunday evening from Reserve duty in Columbus, Ohio, in the Fall of 1980 having been commissioned as a Naval Officer and Chaplain, May 5th, 1980. As I entered the front door, I called out for Connie. The house was strangely silent. She was nowhere to be found. From the basement I heard the murmuring of voices. Slowly, I descended the basement stairs only to discover my wife and the property manager, Ray, in the basement alone in the dark with a flashlight. Well, you can imagine having been married only a few years to a beautiful woman the jealous suspicious thoughts that immediately flooded my mind. "What's

Bethel Lutheran was my first congregation and my first love in the ministry. They are the saints I will always remember and cherish in a very special way. Called to serve their souls with the Gospel, I was their pastor and safely ensconced aboard the flight deck of God's all-sufficient grace. Life was good because God is good.

MAG 29 Active Duty

Blood, Sweat and Tears

I love Marines. I love working with Marines. I love their attitude about life, their "can do" spirit, their "modify, adapt and overcome" war-fighting worldview, their "spit and polish" military mindset, their willingness to sacrifice for the greater good, their fearlessness running into a firefight, their pride in accomplishment and owning-up to responsibility, and their advancement in rank based on merit. No one is given the title of "Marine." You have to earn it, which means every true Marine stands shoulder to shoulder with every other Marine who has ever earned the title. Marines carry their present marching orders back through time to America's Revolutionary war of Independence defending the nation. There are no retired Marines, only Marines no longer serving on active duty. "Semper Fi"[45] to a Marine is more than a slogan, it is a way of life.

Therefore, it was with great excitement that I received my first set of active duty orders directing me to report for duty as the Group

---

going on here?" I demanded.

Ray responded quietly, "Good to see you, Pastor, we've been searching the walls for more signs of bats in the dark and I think we've found some," The explanation sounded reasonable and believable to me, so I bought it. He was right. More bats. The walls were fumigated shortly thereafter. The bats died never to be heard from again. And there would be no future property rendezvous meetings scheduled in the parsonage basement with the lights out.

[45] Semper Fi is short for Semper Fidelis which derives from Latin meaning, "Always faithful," that is, always faithful to the warrior code and the mission of the United States Marine Corps.

Chaplain to the Commanding Officer of Marine Air Group 29 (MAG 29), Jacksonville, North Carolina.[46] MAG 29 was comprised of eight helicopter squadrons at the time: Hueys, Cobras, Sea Stallions and VMO-1. Total company was about 2000 Marines plus their families. The Group Chaplain would be responsible to lead and implement the Command Religious Program under the direction of the Commanding Officer. It was July, 1982. I was ready to go.

I was 32 years old, in top physical shape and ready to train and deploy wherever the Marines would go. With eight Helo squadrons in the Air Group each led by their own CO and XO and I the only chaplain for MAG 29 during my first year of active duty, it meant that the opportunities to deploy with any given squadron were numerous and perpetual. America would not see a major buildup for war until Desert Storm (1990) so most deployments were inside CONUS.[47]

Nevertheless, each deployment which lasted typically a few weeks to a couple of months meant separation time from the wife and kids. Connie and I had been married for only 5 years at the time. We had two young daughters, Amanda (born 1979) and Amy (born 1981). Kim, our third daughter, would be born in 1984 at the Camp Lejeune base military hospital, North Carolina.[48]

Run, run, run. Train, train, train. When the running and training is done there will be more, on that you can depend. Marines always seem to move in double cadence time. The chaplain and his/her RP[49] is part of the team. Where the Marines go, the chaplain follows and

---

46   The Marine Corps has no Doctors, Dentists or Chaplains called to serve from among their ranks. Rather, the Marines, as the premier fighting force of the nation, "steals" all Doctors, Dentists and Chaplains from the Navy to serve alongside the Marines.
47   CONUS stands for: (Within the) CONtinental United States.
48   Total separation time from my family across 25 years of active and reserve duty from 1980 to 2005 with the Navy and the Marine Corps team totaled about six years. During a typical naval career of 20 years approximately 25% will be deployment time.
49   The chaplain is a non-combatant who serves without a weapon. The chaplain is a man of peace in the midst of a mean, lean fighting machine. He has a trained assistant whose Navy rate is called RP, which stands for "Religious Program Specialist." He/she serves alongside the chaplain and carries a weapon ready to fight and kill as necessary.

trains accordingly. Marines PT[50] daily. Three, four and five mile runs are common not to mention the sit-ups, pull-ups and calisthenics done in formation. Appearance is a big deal to a Marine. Not only must you look sharp in uniform but even when you jog in formation you must jog smartly. If your hands are swinging in cadence too high and tight to your chest, it makes you look a bit girly, and you will be corrected. Drop your hands to your waist and keep them there. I can speak from personal experience my first year jogging with Marines.

I loved to jog with Marines. It's an exhilarating feeling of strength to jog in formation on a military base or better yet, down the streets in the local neighborhood right outside of the gates of the base as we did in Algiers, New Orleans.[51] Frequently, many sleepy-headed Crescent City dwellers were rudely awakened by a morning cadence rattling the neighborhood windows shouted out by a bunch of hard chargin' lean, mean Marines. The neighbors loved it. At least they never complained.

One morning after a PT run dosed with perspiration and upon return to my office the muse of inspiration grabbed me and I penned my own cadence for Marines. It went like this:

> Up in the morning with the rising sun
> Gonna run all day till the runnin's done
> Mama and Papa lyin' in the bed
> Papa rolls over and this is what he said:
> Hey, let us pray!
> Twice a day!
> Let us pray!
> Twice a day!
> Our Father
> In the sky

---

50   PT: military acronymn for Physical Training.
51   My last tour of duty was with the 8th Marine Corps Recruiting District, Algiers, New Orleans, LA, 2000-2004. We often jogged on the raised berm of the old railway line parallel to the Mississippi river.

MAG 29 ACTIVE DUTY

> Hear my prayer
> Before I die
> Don't wanna die
> Gonna live!
> Gotta live!
> La-dee, La-dee, La-dee-O
> Well, I don't know but I've been told
> La-dee, La-dee, La-dee-Eee
> Big, bad, lean, green fightin' machine.

I thought without a doubt that my new inspired cadence would be enshrined with the Marine Corps hymn, "The Halls of Montezuma." I was ready, willing and super-charged to lead the chant in formation. Once it caught on, I imagined Marines would be chanting the cadence in the passageway or on the way to the scuttlebutt and certainly in the head. Such tricky lyrics and surreptitiously Christian! But it never caught on, not even given an honorable mention. I wonder why? Oh, well. I guess some things just take time to mellow and penetrate the psyche.

On October 23rd, 1983, Pearl Harbor struck again. A lone, fanatical, maniacal Muslim terrorist raced his half-ton pick-up truck passed the Marine guard shack loaded with the equivalence of 12,000 pounds of TNT where the Marines were bivouacked located at one end of the airport in Beirut, Lebanon. With a hate-filled smirk on his face he drove directly into the narthex of the four story building. The terrorist detonated himself igniting his payload which collapsed the building and tossed 241 souls instantly into eternity. Most of the Marines were still asleep in their racks at 0622 that Sunday morning. Now all were gone, in the twinkling of an eye. President Reagan had sent in the Marines to be peacekeepers hoping to hold at bay the growing civil war in strife-torn Lebanon. The Marines were there for a righteous and a just cause. Now, they were all gone. Where was God? Did He not care?

Could He not have stopped this madness?

I was at the MAG 29 Air Station chapel that Sunday morning ready to begin Sunday morning worship when the word came through that there had been a terrible explosion and large loss of life at the Marine barracks in Lebanon. No one yet knew how bad it was but it would become the greatest single-event loss of life to the Marine Corps since Iwo Jima, February, 1945. What followed at Camp Lejeune and the Marine Corps Air Station in the next few weeks was unbelievable shock, grief, anger and pain.

For the next two to three weeks all chaplains in the area were on restriction for call duty 24/7. As the Marines were excavated from the rubble and their remains identified often through dental records, word was sent back to the states and a CACO[52] call was set up to personally visit the home of the family who had lost a Marine. CACO calls were made around the clock for the next two to three weeks until every last family had been personally and officially notified. Most chaplains and officers who made the CACO calls did not know the family of the Marine prior to the visit.

Burned deep into my memory is one particular CACO call I made to a young wife with four young children who lived in a glorified trailer park at Camp Lejeune called Midway park. It was about 4:30 a.m. when we knocked on the door. We were greeted by a young mother cradling her child in her arms. We entered and sat down on a small couch opposite her. She knew what was coming. We told her that the remains of her Marine had been identified. He had perished in the blast. The young Marine's wife began to cry. One by one the children came out from the back of the trailer, from the youngest to the oldest, all four of them. When they learned that Daddy would not be coming home, their tears were uncontrollable. I remember seeing a crucifix hanging on the wall or was it around the wife's neck? I can't remember,

---

52 CACO is the military acronym for: Casualty Assistance Calls Officer which usually involves an officer and a chaplain in Dress Blues making an official Command visit to the bereaved Marine family in person with the notification that their Marine is not coming home.

but at that moment I spoke to her of God's Gospel of peace and His covenant of love in the midst of this gut-wrenching terrible tragedy. I tried to assure her that through the covenant of baptism her Marine's soul, her husband and the father of her children was not lost and she would see him again in Paradise. Words are nearly impossible at such a time and were difficult to speak in the face of such a tragic cruel ending to life. All that love could cling to now were memories.

President Reagan and Nancy arriving at Camp Lejeune, NC for the Memorial Service for the fallen, November, 1983.

President Reagan comforting the few survivors after the memorial service on a cold, miserable rainy day in November.

The grief was real and palpable written across all the faces of the families who had lost a Marine.

Two days after the Beirut bombing Operation Urgent Fury ordered by President Reagan commenced at dawn on October 25, 1983. Combat raged across the island of Grenada as the armed forces of the United States Army, Navy and Marine Corps engaged the enemy.

In a firefight at Fort Frederick, which was located on the southwest corner of the island, Marine Air Support was called into suppress enemy fire emanating from enemy headquarters. In the assault two AH-1 Cobra attack helicopters, both from MAG 29, Jacksonville, North Carolina, played vital roles in the mission. Both were two-seater aircraft; both were shot down. The one Marine officer that survived, Captain Tim Howard, USMC, had an unbelievable story to tell.[53]

Captain Howard managed to crash land his Cobra now on fire and falling out of the sky after he was badly wounded, his right arm and leg shattered by incoming fire. The jolt from the crash caused Captain Jeb Seagle, his co-pilot, to regain consciousness. Seagle exited the downed

---

53   https://www.mca-marines.org/leatherneck/operation-urgent-fury-grenada. Accessed 3/27/23. Operation Urgent Fury involved about 7,000 military personnel. American forces suffered 19 dead and 150 wounded.

Cobra dragging Captain Tim Howard out and away from the burning wreck to safety. However, they were now both exposed to enemy small arms and machine gun fire. Captain Seagle attended to Howard's wounds and placed a tourniquet on Howard's arm which was bleeding profusely. Realizing that the enemy was quickly approaching, Seagle was ordered by Howard to save himself and get help. Capt. Seagle distracted the enemy by waving his arms and moving away from his stricken pilot. This action bought enough time for a CH 46 helicopter to land, extricate and rescue Howard from a certain death situation.

A second Cobra helicopter piloted by Capt. John Giguere and First Lieutenant Jeff Scharver advanced into the firefight spraying the enemy attackers with machine gun and rocket fire scattering the attackers and thus enabling the rescue operation to succeed. The second Cobra left the hot zone and headed back to the USS Guam but shortly thereafter received incoming heavy enemy anti-aircraft fire and plunged into the sea killing both Marines.

By Capt. Seagle's extraordinary courage under fire, uncommon valor and devotion to duty, he assured that his fellow Marine would be rescued. Tragically, however, Capt. Seagle was captured and executed by the enemy. His body was found on the beach where he fell. For his extraordinary actions and heroism that day,

Captain Seagle dragging Captain Howard from his burning Cobra helicopter to safety. From a painting of the incident formerly displayed on the walls of the Pentagon. https://www.combatreform.org/grenada.htm (accessed June, 2023)

Captain Seagle was awarded the Navy Cross posthumously. Back home at MAG 29 there would be more CACO calls, more grief, more tears, and a memorial service to honor the dead.

What do you think? Is baptism into Christ Jesus mere ritual? Something done in infancy and quickly forgotten? Had these Marines been baptized by water into Christ at some time in their life before they deployed to Beirut? Before the Granada invasion? Captain Jeb Seagle was born and raised a Missouri-Synod Lutheran. From my experience ministering to Marines I can almost guarantee to you that 90% of them were already baptized. Then why didn't God protect them? Could not His almighty hand have prevented this? Most assuredly, but you must also understand that God did protect them. He did keep His word. Through baptism into Christ Jesus, God made their souls invulnerable no matter what happened to their bodies. Scripture promises to all, "He that believes and is baptized shall be saved." Mark 16:16.

Awake or at sleep, baptism hides your soul, your true life, the real you, away in the heart of Christ Jesus where no act of war, violence or terrorism can touch you. This is what the Lord has promised every baptized believer. Baptism grants eternal hope and can make you fearless in the face of any danger. Baptism gives you the strength to pick up your boots and do your duty one step at a time by placing them securely in the footprints of God according to the script He has already written for your life. These Marines did their duty for God and country. They completed His script. Do you believe this?

Helo Down Over I-95

Threading the eye of the needle.

We were falling out of the sky at 1000 feet, or Angels One, as military pilots would say. The control panel on the Huey lit up like a

HELO DOWN OVER I-95

Christmas tree. Flashing lights, shrill buzzers and the grinding sound of metal gears filled my helmet. Both side doors on the Marine Corps Huey helicopter were wide open and the ground was coming up fast. I was the chaplain riding in the back seat with two Marine Corps pilots at the controls.

We banked hard to port. The farmer's fields of South Carolina, freshly ploughed and soft from heavy rains the night before were coming up fast. Perhaps this will be a "soft" crash landing in a pile of mud, I thought and hoped for an instant, but instead the Marine pilots circled back over Interstate 95 and brought the Huey down to about three feet off the ground with the intention to use the grassy median strip as a potential runway. They then piloted the Huey forward like a plane threading the needle between trucks, tractor-trailers and cars rushing past on either side of a four-lane highway. Without exaggeration, the tip of the spinning rotor blades could not have been more than three feet distance from the passing trucks.

As we were moving forward, still three feet off the ground, I could see through the cockpit windshield a concrete overpass and high tension wires quickly approaching. Major Lee piloted the Huey forward, closer and closer, heading straight for the concrete overpass ahead. About twenty feet from the overpass he finally landed the Helo on the median strip grass, shut down the engines and three helmeted men in green flight suits popped out of the Huey. The roar of the non-stop traffic almost drowned out our voices.

"Major, what happened up there?"

"Chaplain, we lost hydraulic pump number one. When that happens usually the second pump follows quickly. If that happens we lose all ability to steer the aircraft so I wanted to be moving this way forward (motioning with his hands, straight and level) and not this way hovering down (motioning again with hands in a downward spiral).

"Besides, Chap, what do you see on the top of that hill?"

"I looked up and said, "Motel Six, Major."

He said, "Yes sir! That's where we're staying tonight . . . and I didn't want to walk too far!"

True story, every bit of it. Love those Marines. Always ready. Always trained. Consider this simple truth. I am alive today because of their Marine Corps training that conditions every Marine to overcome the urgent impulse to panic in a crisis or surrender when overwhelmed by threatening immediate circumstances. Consider also this that both Marine pilots and of course, the chaplain had been baptized into Christ Jesus. God was keeping up His end of the baptismal covenant that day just as He had promised in Scripture,

> "For He shall give His angels charge over you to keep you in all your ways. In their hands they shall bear you up, *lest you fall out of the sky at Angels One and crash on the median strip below.*" Psalm 91: 11, 12.

Above is my simulated photo shop recreation of our "crash" landing on I-95 somewhere over South Carolina enroute to MCAS, Jacksonville, North Carolina.

Okay, so it's not an exact quote from the good book but it's close in spirit! The promise of God covers all earthly circumstances. Besides, wouldn't you expect to find Angels hovering port and starboard near the tips of the Huey rotor blades spinning above the ground at 1,000 feet? They were there that day and the Marines slept well that night. These Marine pilots literally threaded the eye of the needle that day landing on the cramped "flight deck" of the I-95 median strip. It was a good day to be alive.

Unbridled Ambition

> *"Ambition leads me not only farther than any other man has been before me, but as far as I think it possible for man to go."*[54]

In the immortal words of country singer Jerry Reed, "When you're hot, you're hot!" My brain was on fire orbiting in the rarefied space of erudite and perspicacious theological constructs since graduating from the seminary in 1977. I was itching to get back into academics. I had been turned on to the Hebrew language the last year of seminary with its powerful but simple syntax and began to imagine myself living out the career of an OT professor teaching at one of our seminaries. To acquire a PhD in Hebrew and Semitic languages and become tenured as an OT professor was a place that few pastors of the LCMS would dare to go. What honor would be mine! How the students would look up to my dazzling and scintillating interpretation of Scripture! How the students would be amazed at the depth of my erudition, and drool over their pens to capture my every thought on paper! At that time in my

---

[54] From the diary of James Cook, 1728-79, English explorer whose cartographical skills and superb seamanship mapped out in great detail the island land masses of New Zealand, Australia and Hawaii. https://www.brainyquote.com/quotes/james_cook_188518?src=t_ambition. (accessed May, 2023).

life, the difference between holy godly ambition and simply being "full of it" was indistinguishable. Knowledge without love for the student is overweening hubris; love for the student dispensed without knowledge is overweening laziness. Neither hubris nor laziness profits anyone in any vocation.

Dr. Walter Maier Sr., the founder of The Lutheran Hour and PhD graduate of Harvard in OT languages and literature epitomized in my mind the perfect career path.[55] I had taken five courses at the seminary under his son, Dr. Walter Maier Jr, affectionately called WAM by his students because of his rapid fire of speaking and I loved every minute of class. If I could find the way to fund such a degree, I believe God had given me enough brain power to achieve the goal. The military offered the opportunity.

Upon entering active duty in 1982, any service member could pay into Veterans Assistance Education Program (VEAP)[56]. After two years of active duty with an honorable discharge the service member could then receive a pay-out to pursue a college education or advanced degree. This ulterior motive and benefit became my main strategy to re-enter the academic world and eventually land a position as a professor in one of our two seminaries. My "superior" brain had figured out all of God's footprints in advance that I would need to achieve success. I was a step ahead of God and writing my own script. Surely, God would be pleased with my plans because after all it was all church work. I would do it all for His name's sake. What could possibly go wrong? God would bless every footprint that I had so carefully designed. Me and God, in that order, were really tight, so I thought.

Toward the end of the second year of active duty, the chaplain has

---

55   I had taken general linguistics classes and Ugarit at the University of Pittsburgh, 1981-82. I also dabbled in introductory Arabic through a correspondence course at the University of Wisconsin, 1985.

56   The VEAP program in the 80s offered a $2 to $1 assistance plan for education post military service. The service member could contribute up to a max of $2700 thereby acquiring $5400 for education. VEAP has been replaced by the Post-9/11 GI Bill which offers much greater enhancements than its predecessor and enabled me to substantially pay for 80% of the cost of my PhD program at CTSFW from 2015-2020.

to decide whether to continue on active duty or return to reserve duty and civilian life. I chose the latter. It wasn't that I hated active duty, I loved it and I fit in well with the military mindset but unbridled ambition reigned in my heart that just had to be scratched. Academia called. I had to respond. After three years as the Group chaplain for MAG-29 I left active duty voluntarily and returned to the seminary in the summer of 1985 to pursue my dream of becoming an OT professor.

We packed our bags, and downsized most of our household furniture. I sold my piano of 27 years and we headed for St. Louis. Connie and our three young daughters crammed our remaining belongings and piles of my books into an old two bedroom, roach-infested apartment building on San Bonita drive.[57] The seminary owned the whole block of apartments contiguous with seminary property. Many graduate and married students lived there. I was back in academia, certain I was standing in the footprints of God. I was back in the classroom, ready to hit the books, get the degree and set the world on fire. Midnight lucubrations and the pursuit of theological treasure hidden away in the endless stacks of library books gave my heart powerful palpitations. The smell of rare musty books in the library would soon fill my nostrils once again. Life was good, very good!

Advanced degrees in the Lutheran church do not come easy. Before one can enter a doctoral degree program the candidate must acquire the STM (Master of Sacred Theology) degree first which is intended to weed out the dreamers from the earnest seekers. I had applied for admission and had been accepted into the School for Graduate Studies.[58] Now I sat back in the classroom again just eight years after acquiring the M.Div. with students only a few years younger than I. It was an exhilarating experience to be immersed in books, studies, the Seminary

---

57 Since our 10 month stay in the apartment (from July 1985 to April 1986), the seminary sold the properties years ago and built new, clean marriage housing units on campus with spacious rooms and modern conveniences. It was a vast improvement over the old San Bonita apartments. Thank God for some foresight, wisdom and donor's money.

58 See Appendix 1, my letter of acceptance for Graduate Studies dated April 24, 1984.

library, notes, exams and dedicated Lutheran confessional professors. This is what I wanted. My plan had succeeded thus far. I knew God would carry me across the finish line.

I quickly discovered that the seminary environment was a culture shock far removed from whoosh-whoosh-whoosh of helicopters, deployments, weapons of war, constant PT, constant counseling, CACO calls and the daily earthy rough and tumble experience of Marine Corps culture. How soon I would miss it! But I had to stay focused, greater footsteps that I had carefully planned were in my future.

In April of 1985, three months before discharge from my first tour of active duty, I received my initial financial aid award letter stating that I had received a full-tuition graduate study grant for the academic year 1985-86. After only two months on campus, I hit the first speed bump to my academic dreams. I was informed that the grant money was given conditionally, quarter by quarter, depending upon the previous quarter's grades. In the Fall of '85, new grant reward "goalposts" were announced. For an A- average, the candidate would receive a ½ tuition grant. For an A average, the candidate would receive a full tuition grant. I didn't like the additional pressure but I figured I could handle it.

Mid-way through the Winter quarter (1985-86), I received a Christmas present direct from the financial aid office. I was called into the office and told that because I was a graduate from the "other seminary"[59] which they had "just discovered" reviewing my records therefore I was no longer eligible for any further grants or scholarships until I completed the STM degree at St. Louis. This was due to the fact that the donor for all graduate scholarships and grants, the W. Scheele foundation, which funds the entire graduate studies program,

---

59   For decades the Synod had considered the St. Louis seminary, its faculty and students, as the theological cornerstone of the Synod. The Fort Wayne seminary with its historical roots in Springfield, Illinois, was always considered the "practical" seminary churning out qualified pastors to be sure but not nearly as theologically polished as St. Louis grads. Today, those stereotypes have all but evaporated. CTSFW generates superb pastors supported by a highly educated faculty, holding many doctoral degrees, enhanced by a new multi-million dollar library on campus.

stipulated that its grant money will only go to St. Louis grads, not Fort Wayne grads.[60]

A Niagara cataract of roaring ice water suddenly froze all my academic ambitions. I complained. I griped. I rattled every cage. I took my case all the way to Dr. Karl Barth's office, then acting president of Concordia Seminary, St. Louis, all to no avail. That I was a Fort Wayne graduate and not a St. Louis graduate was plain on my initial application and every subsequent correspondence with the graduate school. I was hiding nothing.

I soon discovered I wasn't alone. Other Fort Wayne grads who were also in the STM program with me were offered the same deal. It was a bitter pill. All my financial plans to survive graduate school with Connie and our three young daughters without incurring great debt were quickly eviscerated. Our savings from active duty, the VEAP program, and a monthly check from participation in the Naval Reserve still fell short of necessary expenses. I had to take out $7500 in student loans to survive the school year. I was angry. Who wouldn't be? I had uprooted my family, moved half-way across the country, stuffed everything we owned into a dingy two-bedroom apartment and probably kicked any future Navy Career out the door for good.

I do not write these words harboring latent revenge or to expose my church body to criticism or any form of litigation. My point is not to prove that I was right and unfairly treated and they were wrong. At the time, I did not discern the footsteps of God for my life as He had promised. What guided my heart was unbridled ambition seeking a place of honor in the church in order to display my theological erudition which I was hiding under the rags of arrogant humility. I see that now. I didn't see it then.

I had launched my own flight. I had written the script for my own mission without regard for the rest of ship's company, that is, the saints of God. Bitterness and disappointment were the contrails that filled the

---

60   See Appendix 2: My letter to Chaplain Campbell, Dr. Robert Preus and his response to me.

sky in the wake of my headstrong flight path. Nevertheless, God has His way of getting us back on track. I was still baptized into His covenant. My heady willfulness had not done irreparable harm that He could not repair. A new "meatball" suddenly appeared in my vision on the horizon. The next immediate and necessary step was to secure the proper glide slope. It would take a few more anxious months to land safely on His celestial flight deck but safely land, I did, by the grace of God.

Recalled!

> *The light of the eyes rejoices the heart,*
> *and good news refreshes the bones.*[61]

Good news is a tree of life to those who receive it. Good news conquers the past. Good news seizes the rich golden horizon of promise. I had good news, no, I had great news, no, I had extraordinary news! In the midst of my defeats and setbacks in graduate school after forcing myself into the academic world and seeing the light of success flicker, fade and burn out in my self-conceived theological tunnel, I had applied for reentry to active duty. Perhaps, I had been mistaken about the future. Perhaps, a professorship was not in the cards, or to be more precise, the life of a seminary professor had not been written into the script of God's footsteps for me. I still longed for active duty. The military culture suited my personality just fine. It had been a comfortable shoe for me. Maybe my willing feet would be given another chance.

1985 slipped into 1986. It would prove to be the best January of my life, so far. President Reagan was half way through his second term of office after a massive 49 state landslide victory. America was back. Patriotism was high. Vietnam was in the rearview mirror. The Russian bear was growling but Reagan was more than up to the task.

---
61   Proverbs 15:30.

RECALLED!

With the cold war in full throttle, President Reagan, the great communicator, displayed his eloquence by raising American hearts to envision themselves as a "shining city on a hill." Unabashedly, Reagan portrayed America as the best beacon of hope to conquer any tyranny and put down any dictatorship. America can and should blaze a bright trail into the horizon of peace, honor and righteousness for all the nations of the world. But no matter how many eloquent words it may take to stir the human heart, the reality is that we still live and breathe in a sinful fallen world. Words must be backed by strength, that is, military strength or the bully on the street will call you out, humiliate you and make you pay. Reagan knew this and so did his administration. America's defense budget after years of decline was dramatically and consistently increased to meet worldwide threats and manage all commitments to our allies.

America's defense budget goal in the 80's was a 600 ship Navy. One of the biggest and brightest stars of the new fleet was a brand new aircraft carrier named after America's most robust President, Theodore Roosevelt. This massive 100,000 ton behemoth, Nimitz class, super carrier became the pride of the fleet when she was christened on October 25, 1986, by Mrs. Barbara Lehman, the wife of Navy Secretary John Lehman at Newport News, Virginia.

October 25th was a dazzling Fall day with light rain and occasional sunbursts in Newport News as the commissioning ceremony began. The military bands quickened the heartbeat of the enormous crowd raising a lump of pride in your throat. The trumpets sounded a clarion call to action. The cymbals clashed in rhythm while the crew of TR manned the rails. Simultaneously, all the ship's bells and whistles pierced the eardrums to signal the birthing to new life of USS Theodore Roosevelt CVN-71[62] in the traditional Navy commissioning ceremony. TR had come alive and what a magnificent ship she was.

---

[62] Hull designations are not random numbers assigned to new ships. C stands for aircraft carrier, V for fixed wing fighter aircraft, N stands for nuclear propulsion and 71 indicates that this is the 71st aircraft carrier hull built and commissioned by the United States Navy, hence, CVN-71.

Fly-over, USS Theodore Roosevelt CVN-71, October 25, 1986. (TR cruise book, 1987.)

CAPT Paul W. Parcells leading the commissioning crowd in 3 cheers for TR. (TR cruise book, 1987.)

Secretary of Defense Caspar W. Weinberger was the principal speaker at the commissioning ceremony. He said, "Theodore Roosevelt was a man of vision and peace, whose policies guided the United States toward the position we now hold—the world's most powerful defender of freedom. Nothing we as a nation might do to honor Theodore Roosevelt's legacy more appropriately captures his strength of spirit and the force of liberty than this great ship."[63]

It was a big ship and a big deal with many more new ships to come and our enemies knew it. The huge crowd was guesstimated to be about 30,000. The historic presidential yacht, the Sequoia, was parked off TR's stern as a tribute to his legacy. The weekend was filled with festivities and

---

63   https://magazines.marinelink.com/Magazines/MaritimeReporter/198612/content/theodore-roosevelt-commissioned-201619. (accessed October 13, 2022.)

commissioning balls to celebrate the new ship. I know. I was there. I had applied for recall to active duty and through the diligent work of senior supportive chaplains[64] and the growing needs of the Navy not only was I recalled to active duty but I was given orders to serve aboard the nation's newest aircraft carrier, USS Theodore Roosevelt CVN-71.

The original crewmembers who take a new Navy ship out to sea are called "Plank Owners."[65] It's a distinct honor to hold such a title in the Navy. Not all chaplains in the Navy get orders to serve aboard a super carrier in their entire career. Not only did I have orders but I was part of the original crew that would take her out to sea and engage in many historic "firsts" in the life of TR.

Now I knew what I wanted in life. The footsteps of God were crystal clear to me. My previous nine months on the campus of Concordia Seminary, St. Louis, were simply a winnowing exercise to sort out and prioritize the desires of my heart for the arduous work and the necessary commitment to Chaplain Corps ministry that lay before me. All I wanted now was a full 20 year active duty career, longer, if possible, by the grace of God. My heart had found its home. I was back on active duty and it was good, so good, to be home.

In 1986 the movie Top Gun was all the rage in the theaters. Perfect timing. It epitomized my gun-ho attitude toward the ministry, toward life and my fellow shipmates. In the 80's the Navy's recruiting slogan was, "Navy. It's not just a job, it's an adventure!" A grand new adventure in my life had just begun. I was super-charged and super-proud to serve aboard a super carrier as an commissioned Navy Lieutenant, Chaplain Corps, and an integral part of TR's crew. What an incredible script God had written for me. Not only would carrier operations on the flight deck come to symbolize in my mind the actions of God on His celestial flight deck for every sanctified baptized Christian life, I was literally standing on the flight deck of a brand new aircraft carrier. Life can be grand indeed.

---

64   See Appendix 3. Letters of support from senior Chaplains Campbell, Lecky and Weeks.
65   See Appendix 5 for original Plank Owner certificate.

Life aboard a Super Carrier

> "Strong as a bull moose and you
> can use us to the limit."
> *TR is underway, September 22nd, 1986.*[66]

USS Theodore Roosevelt, CVN-71, was and still is a magnificent ship in fighting trim. Her battle history is filled with a long-list of superb accomplishments, awards and military engagements. Every mission TR engaged in after her commissioning during my tour of duty was a Navy first. Captain Parcells, TR's first skipper, made us all proud to serve aboard her. Every department aboard TR was ready for any engagement in the spirit of her bull-moose legendary namesake, President Theodore Roosevelt.

I served aboard TR from April 1986 to July 1988, the majority of the time at sea. When I first checked aboard TR and met the Navigator he said to me, "Welcome aboard, Chaplain!" Adding a smirk coupled with an intensive stare he said, "And you can kiss your wife and kids good-bye." I laughed nervously at the exaggeration but it proved to be more than correct. The declared OPTEMPO[67] for TR was every month at sea would be balanced by two months in port. That might have been true for lesser ships of the line between six month deployments but aboard TR even this "downtime" was filled by short excursions of one week to two months at sea for weapons testing, catapult adjustments, hull maneuvers, shock trials and whatever else needed to be tested to make sure we were ready to fight any enemy. Needless to say, the Navigator was right. Most of my tour aboard TR was spent at

---

66 This was the first official message traffic from TR during builders sea trials sent out to all fifteen carriers of the fleet on active duty in the US Navy, September 22, 1986 at 0800 hours. (From TR's first cruise book).

67 Operational Tempo generally refers to the quick response of our fighting forces in a military situation but also refers in general to the ship's scheduled homeported time vis-à-vis the ship's scheduled sea deployment time.

LIFE ABOARD A SUPER CARRIER

sea away from Connie, my wife and our three daughters.[68]

In the Navy there is a well-oiled saying often grunted when deployed, "Haze grey and underway." It is an apt phrase describing not only the frequently grey horizon blending into a restless grey ocean, but the days spent at sea take on the same haze grey coloration in the mind. Everything in the ship appears in various shades of grey. Vibrant colors are absent and every day at sea often feels like every other day at sea.

For a super carrier at sea, the ship never sleeps. There is always some department in full work mode at any hour of the day or night. For the Religious Ministries Department aboard TR, Sunday was the only day that seemed any different from any other day at sea. On Sunday morning the chaplains would offer worship services for the crew. After all, one of the main historical congressional mandates for establishing a Chaplain Corps was to provide for the religious needs of military personnel stationed far from home who are unable to attend church services while deployed. Sunday was our meat, potatoes and gravy day, a fundamental *raison d'être* of our very existence. Every Sunday morning at sea, therefore, a Roman Catholic service and a Protestant service was held in the *fo'c'sle* [69] of the ship. If there was a Jewish, Mormon or a Muslim chaplain aboard, services in these faith-groups would also be offered.

---

68   Chaplain Norvell Knight (Southern Baptist) was the senior chaplain aboard TR when I checked in as the third chaplain to the team. It was his desire as well as Chaplain Ed Condon (Roman Catholic) that the Command Religious Ministries Department (CRMD) should be a shipboard department in its own right which meant standing watch aboard ship. Standing watch was no problem as long as we were at sea, however, after deployment with TR docked at pier side, standing watch meant that every third day while in port I would be spending my nights aboard TR and not at home. Chaplain Knight and Condon could enjoy a phone watch at home. Rank has its privileges but not for the junior chaplain. However, standing watch aboard ship while in port also meant that I could bring my wife and daughters aboard for the evening meal in the Officer's Mess. It was quite a treat especially the soft-served ice cream for the girls. Mandy, Amy and Kimberly (7, 5 and 2 years old in 1986) still remember with fondness to this very day running up and down the passageways in TR, jumping over the knee-knockers and climbing up the ladders to Dad's chaplain office. It was a signature tour of duty. For the entire length of the tour, I felt like I had two wives; TR and Connie. However, there was one big wonderful difference: TR was steel plated, Connie was nice and soft.

69   *Fo'c'sle* (pronounced: Fōk-səl) is shortened Navy-speak for Forecastle which is the forward part of the upper deck of the ship.

The forecastle of TR housed the anchor chain[70] making it the largest available open safe compartment—excluding the hangar bay—to hold services aboard the ship while at sea. If we were lucky, we could usually get the Air Boss to stop flight operations on the flight deck for about 30 minutes on a Sunday morning. This was a great blessing because the noise from catapult launches directly overhead while you were in the *fo'c'sle,* one deck below, could be simply deafening. The problem was that the worship service usually lasted for 45 minutes which meant that some part of the service would likely be drowned out by the ear-splitting bang of the catapult slamming into the end of its tube followed by the roar of jet engines in full throttle leaping off the end of the flight deck. Then the whirring of flight deck machinery would set up for the next catapult launch 30 seconds later. If this occurred while you were preaching, your shipmates would see your lips move but not hear a word you said. The Air Boss was certainly sympathetic to the needs of the chaplain but a Navy warship at sea is a constant buzz of activity, training and honing war-fighting skills. A thirty minute stand-down can seem like an eternity.

What do Marines do when faced with an unpredictable fluid situation? Adapt! Modify! Overcome! If it works for Marines why not preachers at sea?

Frequently, half way through my sermon, flight deck operations would suddenly resume with a deafening roar, an ear-splitting bang followed by the launch of another aircraft thirty seconds later. One Sunday morning it dawned upon me that such ear-splitting theatrics could be put to good use in the Sunday sermon if one could get the timing down. In other words, at any point in the sermon when the preacher was ready to launch into a powerful excursus of God's Word he could simply declare, "Thus saith the Lord!" . . . and then wait a second or two for the catapult launch. The ear-drum splitting whoosh-bang

---

70 Each link in the anchor chain weighs 360 pounds and the entire anchor chain with all links weighs 30 tons. There are two anchor chains in the bow of the ship.

of the catapult would not only jar the listeners into instant hyper-vigilance but would also jolt the hearer into crisp alertness for every word the preacher would say next. After all, when God speaks, one should pay attention! It worked better than three cups of caffeine or a bucket of cold water tossed upon a drunken sailor. It was the Sermon on the Mount on steroids with the US Navy assisting the proclamation of His Word. What civilian preacher in his/her civilian parish could ever claim the same military theatrical accoutrements when delivering the Word of God? Preaching at sea aboard TR was an exciting and an ear-splitting adventure. He who has ears left to hear after a TR *fo'c'sle* sermon, let him hear! God had launched me from the bow of His celestial flight deck, catapulted into a new exciting ministry. The view above and below my heavenly cockpit was grand, simply grand.

Danger Zone

The flight deck is 4.5 acres of pure adrenalin rush.

It was 1986. Top Gun was all the rage in theaters across the country and I was serving aboard the biggest, "baddest" warship in the world. The nukes that TR held within its steeled keeled bosom contained more firepower than all the bombs dropped in WWII. It was an exciting time to be alive on active duty serving aboard the world's largest warship powered by the world's most advanced Navy. The Top Gun anthem belted out by Kenny Loggins' screeching guitar and his jet jockey lyrics defined the moment, the mood of the ship and the nation. Engines revved up to a howlin' roar launched the Tomcats onto the highway, the highway in the sky, paved with danger, the andrenalin rush of excitement and the macho readiness for any dog fight that might ensue.

Jet jockeys are a special breed of warrior with a lifestyle all their own. They live on the edge pushing the red line into overdrive to determine the limits of what man and machine can do. I was proud to serve with them and be their chaplain.

Whenever there is trouble in the world, the first question the President asks is, "Where are the carriers?" America has often kept belligerent nations from destroying their neighbors by simply parking a super carrier in their backyard. It's the same spirit of Theodore Roosevelt who said, "Speak softly and carry a big stick." The American military, may be loved or hated by the nations of the world, but no nation on earth carries a bigger stick. America is still respected for its might and power. If that is not a constant mental adrenalin rush then nothing is.

Whenever I could break away for a few minutes from chaplain duties, I would climb the ladder up the decks inside the island to the conning bridge and watch flight ops in progress at sea. The flame and roar from the F-14 Tomcat afterburners launched against the setting sun was an unforgettable sight. The constant coordinated choreography of the deckhands scrambling across the flight deck to play their support roles from taxi, to set-up, to catapult, to launch was a scenario that had to be repeated in an absolute precise sequence in order to launch a multi-million dollar aircraft off the bow of TR successfully. If one step was missing, or the sequence was mismanaged, accidents and death could occur instantly. The American civilian population tends to think that death and maiming only occur in war and not while a nation is at peace, at sea and performing routine training exercises. Nothing could be farther from the truth. The most dangerous real estate America owns is the 4.5 acres of the crowded flight deck of a super carrier. Even with constant emphasis on safety and safety procedures, accidents did happen aboard TR and in one severe case that I recall, instant loss of life.

It was about 1800 and dusk was settling in. A Grumman C-2 Greyhound had just landed on the flight deck. The C-2 is a twin-engine propellor driven plane used to carry mail, supplies and passengers to carriers at sea. The flight deck hands directed the C-2 toward the island amid-ships in order to feather down, chock the wheels and secure the plane. As the C-2 was being secured with the port engine still feathering, one of the experienced deck hands walked under the wing of the C-2 toward the cockpit with head down as if reading something in his hands. In so doing he walked head first straight into the spinning propeller. Immediately a flight deck mishap was called away on the 1 MC.[71] I raced through TR's passageways, up the ladders and to the flight deck to assist. By the time I arrived, just seconds after the event, the mutilated sailor's body had already been put into a zippered black bag, placed carefully upon a pallet and lowered through the ship's elevator to the mess decks. On the mess deck, TR's XO (Executive Officer, CDR Cross, second in command to Captain Parcells) addressed all the sailors who were eating and stated that a tragic mishap and loss of life had just occurred on the flight deck. He then gave the sailor's name and stated that if you knew this shipmate personally and would like to pay respects, now is the time. Then he motioned to me, standing beside our fallen sailor and said, "Here is the chaplain. If you need to talk with him he is ready and available."

In an instant, life could end through any multitude of mishaps at sea. Unlike parish ministry, where death creeps up with the advancing years of old age and often becomes a slow drip of life's energy ebbing away, whenever there is death and/or dismemberment in the military, the tragedy almost always occurs to our young men and women in the prime of life, in the best of health. They are robust, strong and full of life—until life is suddenly and violently ripped away from their grip.

The crew of TR including the embarked Air Wing numbered over 6,000 personnel aboard one ship. The TR cruise book lists 13 sailors who died during those years, 1986-88. Not all were mishaps at sea but all were young and full of life. Such is the military environment the chaplain finds himself immersed in. I loved it. It was a powerful

---

71   1MC stands for "1 Main Circuit." 1MC is the ship's main public address system amplified loud enough to be heard by all embarked personnel in all internal spaces of the ship and topside simultaneously in order to pass general information, orders, GQ and attention to emergency situations.

challenge ministering to the young men and women of America, learning their language, their machines and at the same time seeking to penetrate their minds with the Gospel of Christ Jesus in a relevant way.

I was now certain and fully convinced that I was in the right place, at the right time, joyfully moving forward in the footsteps that God had laid before me. His script was secure and my baptism into Christ Jesus was the tailhook arrested by the cables of God's grace. I was safe on His flight deck again.

Whiffle Bat and Angels

"Ain't no Mama like a Mama bear robbed of her cubs."[72]

All Red Cross messages while deployed are distributed to the crew via the chaplain's office. Red Cross messages can be good or bad news, ranging from the announcement of the birth of a baby, to delinquent bills, to sickness, accident or death in the family. Aboard a warship the size of USS Theodore Roosevelt with a crew of over 6,000 delivering Red Cross messages to your fellow shipmates was a near daily activity. Whether the news is good or bad, it is easy over time for the Chaplain to become routine and a bit indifferent while delivering a Red Cross message. If the news was tragic, you would do your best to empathize, counsel and pray.[73]

The footsteps of God that we are called to walk in are not only

---

72   Hosea 13:8. A slight paraphrase. In this scripture text God is the Mama bear avenging the sins of His chosen people, Israel. Mama bears in nature are known for their fierce protection of their baby cubs.
73   Romans 12:15. "Rejoice with those who rejoice, and weep with those who weep," is an evangelical command from the hand of the Apostle Paul for all Christian chaplains. Easier written than done! It is always easy to rejoice and celebrate when good news arrives at sea, however, when the news is bad or tragic, empathetic weeping is much more difficult to produce from the heart.

guideposts along the way but Christ-like building vignettes meant to shape our attitudes and behavior to be more like the Master. So when a Red Cross message came across my desk at sea toward the end of a five month deployment in early 1987 with my name on it requiring me to contact Connie immediately back home in Virginia Beach because of a break-in incident, my heart pounded and my mind scrambled for the reason why. I called home through the shipboard MARS radio system.[74]

It appears that the Schreiber household had received an unwanted intruder one Saturday evening around midnight on a cold winter night in January. We had purchased the new model home in the neighborhood about a year earlier. The garage had been furnished and finished as an office for the realtors working the neighborhood. We decided to keep the garage as is and use it as my office and library. It looked real snazzy, fully painted, trimmed out with an overhead skylight and complete with French doors in the place of a garage door. We knew that the glass-paneled French doors were not nearly as secure as a regular garage door but Connie always secured the house every night locking all doors. At the base of the French doors she would place heavy rugs rolled up and other obstacles, just in case.

The night of the break-in Connie was wide awake in the upstairs bedroom. The girls were fast asleep in their bedrooms upstairs when Connie was suddenly alarmed by a sharp bang coming from somewhere downstairs. Connie immediately suspected an intruder and raced to arm herself with a deadly weapon . . . a whiffle bat. It was the only thing she could find quickly. Turning on the hallway light, Connie perched herself on the top of the stairs, armed and ready for

---

[74] MARS stands for Military Auxiliary Radio System and is used by the US Department of Defense as a separate dedicated military communication system for the Army, Navy and Air Force. The Navy/Marine Corps team discontinued its use after 2015. While speaking into the microphone one had to press the trigger, speak, say "Over" at the end of your sentence, then release the trigger in order to hear the response of the person you were talking to. This often led to some hilarious conversations when spouses sometimes misunderstood each other and concluded that somehow their romance must be "Over." As in, "I love you—Over," to which was given the reply, "I love you too—Over and Out."

any would-be intruder that would dare to make the ascent. There ain't no tellin' what a Mama bear will do to protect her cubs! Pity the intruder even if it was just a whiffle bat. She waited and listened, listened and waited. Two hours passed until she became somewhat confident that no intruder was in the house.

The night of the intrusion Connie had secured all the doors as usual before bedtime including locking the inside door leading to my office in the garage. By the time the ordeal was over and Sunday morning had arrived the girls did not know anything of what had happened the night before. Connie just wanted to get out of the house as quickly as possible. When she returned from church, she noticed that the French doors didn't look quite right. She called the police to investigate. Sure enough, their consensus was that a break-in had occurred. The intruder had kicked the door open enough to reach in and pull down the bolts that secure one half of the French doors while pushing on the other side to get in. The rugs prevented easy access but the intruder knocked over a small filing box in the process creating the loud bang that startled Connie the night before. Connie told Mandy, our oldest daughter and eight years old at the time, that Jesus had said to the intruder, "No! You're not coming into this house!" Thank God for whiffle bats and angels. Case solved but no intruder was ever caught and no further crime against the Schreiber household was ever committed.

Now just consider for a moment where that incident could have gone without God's promise of security through our baptismal grace and His holy guardian angels standing watch over our lives 24/7. That Red Cross message for me firmly planted a new round of empathy in my heart for all my shipmates and overwhelming gratitude for a God whose watch over us never ceases and whose almighty arms always protect us. Mizpah.[75]

---

[75] Mizpah is an Old Testament blessing first spoken by Laban to Jacob recorded in Genesis 31:49 where he said, "The Lord watch between you and me when we are out of one another's sight." It is a beautiful benediction that was often used by my mother Ruth over the years as she signed off on birthday and anniversary cards mailed to Connie and I.

Short Skirts, Perfume and High Heels

Surely, absence make the heart grow fonder![76]

Any deployment at sea lasting longer than a few weeks or stretching to several months, had the power to generate genuine homesickness for loved ones back home. Homecoming day was always a grand affair and eagerly anticipated by most. Of course there were always those sailors whose first wife was the Navy and when deployed their motto was, "Our of sight, out of mind." However, for the vast majority of the crew homecoming meant that first long kiss with your wife surrounded by your children's clinging hugs. The emotional high that homecoming generated for any Navy ship, whether returning from peacetime operations or a war zone was always an emotional adrenalin love rush.

TR was a huge ship at 100,000 tons. Coming into port at Norfolk until fully docked at pier two was a slow affair usually taking the better part of an hour or more. It always amazed me as TR came into sight of land how vibrant and alive all the colors on shore appeared to be. Weeks and months of "haze grey and underway" aboard ship dulled the visual senses and seemed to fade every color into shades of black and white. But now the trees and grass were the deepest green and the sky azure blue while the buildings, water towers and bill boards seem to explode with dazzling colors. When the gang plank was lowered at pier number two and the crew of TR was called away to disembark, haze grey melted away into a brilliant kaleidoscope of color. It reminded me of the magical transformation in the opening black and white scenes of "The Wizard of Oz" when Dorothy first exited her tornado wrecked home stepping onto the yellow brick road and entered the splash of

---

76   A timeless truth first spoken in Latin by the Roman poet Sextus Aurelius Propertius (b. 50 BC) and later rephrased by James Howell (1650) and then again by Thomas Bayly (1797-1839). The intensity of true love grows in proportion to the distance and the time between the lovers until reunited again. For the interested reader, go to: https://idiomorigins.org/origin/absence-makes-the-heart-grow-fonder. (accessed 05/09/23).

living colors in the land of Oz.

The flight deck of TR stood 60 feet above the water line. On the pier below huddled together were all the TR families of the crew waiting to catch a glimpse of their TR sailor descending the gang plank. Even at 60 feet above the waterline and probably 100 feet from the nearest spouse, I could smell perfume in the air. It was an intoxicating moment and the longer the deployment had been, the greater the intoxication.

When you first descended the gangplank it took a few seconds for situational awareness to set in. Everyone seemed to be yelling, "Over here! We're over here!" but it was hard to discern the voice of your wife and kids even if you had spotted them from the top of the gang plank because as you descended onto ground level all voices and faces melted into one. For a short guy like me, finding your wife and kids in the moving crowd was an sizable challenge but a challenge I eagerly embraced. As I jostled about in the midst of the crowd it was impossible not to inhale the cloud of perfume that hung everywhere, nor was it possible not to see all the make-up, short skirts and high heels the women were wearing. They were dressed to kill, with love, that is.

Dodging and navigating through the perfumed crowd, I, at last, found Connie and the girls. Our eyes locked on each other and we embraced. Our first kiss and embrace was like honeymoon all over again. Oh, what a feeling! Home at last! The kids were ecstatic. Connie was ecstatic. I was ecstatic. Ecstasy reigned!

As we drove home, I held Connie's hand. Everywhere, the intensity of the colors surrounding me flooded my mind as if someone had just replaced the old black and white TV with the latest HD color version. The smile on Connie's face brought more peace and comfort to my heart than I imagined possible and confirmed the words of an old proverb, "Absence makes the heart grow fonder." It sure does. Short skirts, high heels, and perfume may have been the package but most importantly two hearts were united as one once again. The footsteps of

God had led me to this beautiful woman, Connie, more than ten years ago. I could not have asked for a better Navy wife. As we drove away from the parking lot, homesickness swiftly retreated in the rear view mirror of our Safari van. No bolter here just swift recovery on the flight deck of God's love.

Dependents Day Cruise

*"Our country **is** something to be proud of, something to celebrate."*[77]

Saturday, March 14th, 1987. TR was at sea about 100 miles off the coast east of Norfolk, Virginia, for a Dependent's Day cruise. TR had a very special audience that day. Thousands of family members had embarked aboard ship at pier two and were now crowding the bow of the ship forward of the island. Their hearts and minds were bursting with pride for their sons and daughters, the crew of USS Theodore Roosevelt.

A sharp cold icy wind swept over the flight deck while the plane handlers maneuvered the F-14 Tomcats into position for a catapult shot off the angle deck. Typical exercise for the crew but this day was different. All eyes were on their performance. Mom and Dad, brother and sister, wife and kids were all watching.

The CAT jerked the Tomcat forward down 300 feet of flight deck accelerating the fighter jet to 160 mph in two seconds. Incredible. The

---

[77] William J. Bennett. *Why We Fight*. (Washington DC: Regnery Publishing, Inc. 2002), 162, 63. Bennett, former distinguished Secretary of Education under President Reagan, continues, "Why should we shrink from saying so? A sober, a sophisticated, study of our history demonstrates beyond cavil that we have provided more freedom to more people than any nation in the history of mankind; that we have provided a greater degree of equality to more people than any nation in the history of mankind; that we have created more prosperity, and spread it more widely, than any nation in the history of mankind; that we have brought more justice to more people than any nation in the history of mankind; that our open, tolerant, prosperous, peaceable society is the marvel and envy of the ages."
What more could be added? This kind of pride is wholesome, extroverted, and altruistic placing the safety and prosperity of others before self. God bless the USA.

Connie, me, Mom and Dad on TR flight deck.

Dependents on TR flight deck. TR cruise book, 1987.

DEPENDENTS DAY CRUISE

Launch and recovery operations on the flight deck of TR during the dependents day cruise. TR cruise book, 1987.

Dad and Neil posing in front of a F-14 Tomcat after flight operations on Dependent's Day cruise.

F-14 roared off the flight deck, leaping heavenward with full afterburners aflame. Seconds later the Tomcat circled back for an ear-splitting low overhead pass. It was a scintillating display not only military power but of unshakeable trust in man and machine.

The 4.5 acres of a super-carrier flight deck is the most dangerous real estate in America and a most dangerous place to be standing during flight operations. No room for error. The margins of safety are tight, very tight. Strung across the flight deck are four steel cables one of which must be caught by the tailhook of the descending and approaching F-14 Tomcat. Not only could a bolter cause a veer-off into the crowd but these steel cables could snap and break when trapping a jet. If a cable broke, it would fly across the flight deck like an angry coiled steel snake with deadly speed and unpredictability cutting down anything or any pair of legs that stood in its way. The danger zone was not only in the sky but on the flight deck as well. Nevertheless, the Navy was assured and confident that no such mishap would occur at sea during the dependent's day cruise, and it did not.

Neil, my older brother, who serve two tours of combat in Vietnam, was aboard TR that day. He was impressed, really impressed. For years afterward he would tell me it was one of the coolest days of his life. To have Neil on board together with my family and Mom and Dad, who served as a Pharmacist's Mate throughout WWII, was quite a thrill for me as well. There is a snobbish kind of pride that borders on arrogance and goes before a fall, as Scripture tells us, but there is better kind of pride born out of hard work, discipline and accomplishment. That's the kind of pride the Navy put on display for its Navy family. That day I was proud, very proud to be a Chaplain, a Naval Officer and a plank owner serving aboard the Navy's newest aircraft carrier and warship. I was walking in the footsteps of God chosen for me from the day of my baptism into Christ Jesus. His footsteps were exciting. His script for my life simply exhilarating. As far as I was concerned my vocation to serve as a Navy chaplain could last for the next twenty years or more and I would

LT Schreiber, Chaplain Corps, United States Navy, on the quarter-deck of USS Theodore Roosevelt. CVN-71.

be ecstatically happy. I prayed fervently that it would. My tailhook was firmly planted and caught on the flight deck of His expansive grace.

Pass Over

Nothing begins, and nothing ends, that is not paid with a moan. For we are born in other's pain, and perish in our own.[78]

A twenty year active duty career followed by a monthly military retirement check for life is guaranteed to no one who enlists or receives

---

[78] Francis Thompson, 1859-1907, English Poet, cited from the love poem "Daisy." https://agapeta.art/2020/11/20/daisy-by-francis-thompson/. (accessed May, 2023) Thompson is most famously known for his poem entitled, "The Hound of Heaven," which describes God's relentless pursuit of the sinner fleeing His saving grace. For glosses on the sometime archaic usage of the English language used in the 182 verses of "The Hound of Heaven" poem, go to: http://poetry.elcore.net/HoundOfHeavenInRtTGlossed.html. (accessed 05/09/23).

an officer's commission. Your first set of orders begins the winnowing process. The military is a meritocracy. You must earn the next rank and be promoted over your peers every step of the way in order to reach the retirement goal of twenty good years consisting of either active or reserve duty or a combination of both. This means that every commissioned officer within this military meritocracy is given two chances to compete with his/her peers before a promotion board who will then select the best candidates to be promoted to the next highest rank. This includes the chaplain corps.

All officers in their careers are evaluated by their immediate senior officers in the chain of command through regular FITREPS[79] which details their fitness for duty and potential for promotion and command within the Navy. In this way the Officer Corps becomes a pyramid structure with all officers beginning their careers at the bottom of the pyramid starting in their junior ranks. Promotion boards select the best officers to rise to the top based upon their level of competence as compared to all other officers in the same rank and rating throughout the Navy. In a meritocracy the cream rises to the top. Those who twice fail to select for the next rank are released from active duty ending the chance for a full active duty career. The passed over officer usually has the option of continuing his career in the Reserves.

Considering the toil, the struggle and the great expense the nation goes to defend itself against all adversaries and our way of life, the military wants the best of the best to lead from the front with the most capable military hardware on the face of the earth. And considering the multi-billion dollar price tag on America's war machines and the tremendous responsibilities inherent in the nation's profession of arms, I'm sure you would agree. Mediocrity is not a virtue to be promoted in America's military armed forces. Nevertheless, everyone, regardless of race or background has an equal competitive chance to rise to the

---

79 FITREPS is a Navy acronym that stands for Fitness Reports which measure and evaluates the officer's fitness and performance of duty. These reports are the substantial measure of comparison against his/her peers when considered for promotion to the next higher rank.

top in his/her rating and military specialty from the very beginning of their career.

I was gung-ho the Navy/Marine Corps team.[80] My life was now firmly settled in the footsteps of God living out His baptismal grace via the "orders" to serve aboard TR as a chaplain and plank owner. Life was good, real good. The military life suited me just fine. I eagerly looked forward to a bright and prosperous future in the Navy Chaplain Corps.

A little more than half way through my tour aboard TR the LCDR[81] Chaplain Corps promotion board results were published to be implemented the next fiscal year. The promotion flow rate from LT to LCDR Navy wide was generally around 85 per cent in the 1980s. Unless you really screwed up as a Lieutenant, the odds were greatly in your favor that you would be pinning on the LCDR gold leaf collar device soon. Besides, President Reagan's goal was a 600 ship Navy by the end of his term in 1988. The Navy was rapidly expanding and in need of more officers not less.

When January 1987 rolled around and the promotion board results were released, you can imagine how shocked and dismayed I was not to see my name on the promotion list. What in the world had happened? Yes, I still had a second shot at the next promotion board, but to be non-select on any board is a big hit and lessens the chances considerably for success the next time around.

---

80 The Marine Corps is the smallest manned unit within the branches of the Armed Forces with about 190,000 personnel as authorized by Congress. As a result the Marine Corps "borrows" Navy Doctors, Dentists and Chaplains to serve in Marine Corps billets. When a chaplain is given orders to serve with Marines he/she quickly learns to adapt to the Marine Corps culture which includes strenuous PT, strict protocol and a no-nonsense approach to ministry. For the 25 years of my career (active and reserve duty), the majority of my time was spent with Marines and I loved every minute of it.

81 LCDR—Rank of Lieutenant Commander. I began my tour aboard TR as a Lieutenant. The next ranks in ascending order are: Lieutenant Commander (LCDR), Commander (CDR) and Captain (CAPT). The promotion flow between ranks is usually 5-7 years depending upon congressional authorization for the fiscal year which determines the number of officers billets allowed in the ranks for that year and the actions of previous promotion boards. Every officer knew when he/she was coming into the zone for promotion and paid meticulous attention to his/her FITREPS and officer records in order to put the best foot forward before the promotion board.

I counseled with other fellow senior chaplains. I had my record reviewed again and again for accuracy. All my FITREPS were outstanding "water-walking" reports from my previous commands. There were no major hiccups, hits or discrepancies. The consensus from senior chaps seemed to be that since I voluntarily left the Navy after my first tour of duty in order to pursue graduate studies, I had in effect missed out on a couple more FITREPS that could have been in my record had I continued on active duty. My break in service for nine months set me apart from my fellow chaplains regardless of the reason. That probably meant that when my promotion board compared the records of chaplains up for promotion to LCDR, if one chaplain has 10 outstanding FITREPS and the other chaplain has 8 outstanding FITREPS, all other things being basically equal the chaplain with the greater number of outstanding FITREPS and no break in service will be promoted over the other. The records of all military promotion boards are confidential meaning than the reasons for selection or non-selection are not transparent to the officer under consideration nor can they be divulged. Perhaps the counsel of my senior chaplains was right, perhaps not. It seemed logical to me but to this day I will never know.

Life goes on. Now it appeared that God's footsteps were in jeopardy. Why had He recalled me to active duty with the choicest of assignments in the first place? Only to be passed over for promotion? Had I boltered off the flight deck again? I thought my life was settled in the chaplain corps for the next twenty years but the race wasn't over yet. One more chance. One more promotion board. I would give it my best shot.

I did not turn sour toward life or the Navy after my first pass over. I was still serving aboard the biggest warship in the ocean, most of the time at sea and with a proud crew. There was a whole lot in life to be thankful for. The script of God was still good and I did everything in my power in the ministry to assure outstanding

PASS OVER

FITREPS would be included in my record for the next promotion board, and they were.

One year later in early January, 1988, I was driving home from TR in mid-afternoon. TR had been homeported for a few weeks and beside me on the car seat was the new list of chaplains from my second promotion board to be promoted to the next rank of Lieutenant Commander. My name was not on the list. I don't know what I said to Connie as I entered the house but I went upstairs to our bedroom, sat on the edge of the bed and wept. My mind was flooded with anger, resentment and grief. How could this have happened? I gave it my best shot. I was hardly an incompetent chaplain or Naval Officer yet my active duty career was over. Complete failure. After being twice non-select for the next rank by the promotion board, the officer will be discharged from the ranks of active duty soon thereafter. Those were the rules. I knew the rules. I agreed to the rules. There was no real recourse for appeal. The reasons for non-select from any promotion board are strictly confidential. Game over.[82]

I was angry with God. I was angry at life. I was embarrassed to be with fellow chaplains on active duty who would now label me with the pass over stigma as one who never did quite measure up to the rest of us. It hurt bad, real bad. It hurt like hell. For a man his identity is primarily wrapped up in his life's vocation. His vocation is his life and his identity. His life's work defines so many aspects of his personality and his future. God's footsteps had utterly failed me. No tailhook caught on the arresting gear just a plunge into the angry sea. Maybe in the great wisdom of God He had better plans for me "somewhere . . . out there." Maybe He did but I was unaware of them.

Connie held me tight. We wept together for a long time but it would take more time, a good deal more time for the anger and the bitterness to subside to controllable levels.

Shortly after my non-select, TR was deployed at sea again for a few

---

82 "A man's steps are from the Lord, how then can man understand his way?" Proverbs 20:24.

months. It was the summer of 1988. Before I flew off the flight deck of TR in a C-2 headed for home-port to be involuntarily discharged from active duty, I recall having a brief meeting with the Skipper. We met in his ship board office and he wished me the usual good luck and Godspeed. He asked about my future plans and family. He thanked me for my service as chaplain to the crew aboard TR.

CAPT Parcells was sincere and supportive. I greatly appreciated it. But after I returned the thanks, I drifted into a few comments about how life can be basically unfair despite one's best efforts. No sooner had the words exited my mouth than I was soundly rebuked for my thoughts. "Life *isn't* unfair," the Captain asserted, "The promotion board did its due diligence and you came up short against your peers for whatever reason."

So that was that and that was all it was ever going to mean. His words were a slap in the face and a bucket of cold water simultaneously, but it did me a world of good. Whatever the future holds—the Skipper's words in essence were saying—you're not going to play the victim with me as you leave my ship. I heard him loud and clear. Furthermore, I learned that day, if I would take his advice to heart and proceed smartly I would not play the victim at my next duty station in the Naval Reserves or in church ministry, regardless of the nature of any footprint that would drop from Heaven for me. It's a hard lesson in life to learn, real hard.

The propeller driven C-2 was being readied into position for a catapult shot off the flight deck. The time to leave TR had arrived. I exited the island structure on the starboard side of the ship and walked toward the plane. Before climbing the short ladder to board the C-2, I turned backed toward the island, dropped my sea-bag in hand, and facing the Air Boss and the CO, I saluted smartly, and departed.

Guardian Lutheran Church, Jacksonville, Florida

O Lord God, I am indeed unworthy of the office and ministry in which I am to make known Thy glory and to nurture and to serve this congregation. . . if Thou art pleased to accomplish anything through me, to Thy glory and not to mine or the praise of men, grant me, out of Thy pure grace and mercy a right understanding of Thy Word and that I may also, diligently perform it.[83]

God is in the character building business, always has been, always will be. His intent for our life is not just a vague indolent otiose faith in the cross of Christ and the Resurrection to be cashed in when we die so that in this life we can just run around for the rest of our days doing whatever we please. No, of course not. This is why God must trap us again and again on the flight deck of His restraining grace or let us bolter for another go around till we get it right.

His intent for each Christian life, young and old, from cradle to grave, is to shape that life and make it Christ-like thereby becoming a true authentic disciple. This is a non-stop life-long process whether you are aware of it or not. To this the words of Scripture agree:

A disciple is not above his teacher, nor a servant above his master. It is enough for a disciple that he be like his teacher, and a servant like his master.

Matthew 10: 24, 25.

---

83   Luther's sacristy prayer hanging on the wall in my home office above my desk.

Our main problem in life is that we only want His footsteps of joy, not footsteps of sorrow. Our fervent prayer is, "Give me the footsteps of pleasure, O Lord. Forget the footsteps of pain or at least minimize them as much as You can." With such an attitude bitterness and resentment is guaranteed for the Christian. You will soon blame the Almighty because He did not follow the script for your life that you had written and expected for yourself. Certainly God is mightier and stronger than we, we mumble often through clenched teeth, but is He smarter too? Do we not know what is best for our own life? Aren't we the captain of our own destiny? The creator of our own fate? Heaven's answer slaps us down on the flight deck of our arrogance and shouts, "No, No, No, and again, No!" Then, God in His mercy, commences to squeeze your life through the eye of the needle, the impossible task made possible by grace alone, until a Christ-like heart is fashioned within you and carried through all your future days of joy and sorrow.

Forced to leave active duty for failure to select for promotion doesn't mean that the chaplain is divorced or unfit for parish ministry. The Lord's work must go on. In this case in a different vineyard. I submitted my name to several District Presidents within my denomination, The Lutheran Church—Missouri Synod, and soon thereafter received a call to be the pastor of Guardian Lutheran Church, Jacksonville, Florida.

Because our Synod values the parish ministry so highly and does a superb job of cranking out competent and educated Lutheran pastors from both seminaries, the average LCMS pew-sitter believes parish ministry is the pinnacle of all ministries within the church. I disagree. There are many ministry venues where doing the Lord's work places the servant of the Lord in difficult, often dire or dangerous venues such as overseas missionaries in or near war-torn countries, the VA chaplaincy, prison ministry and certainly chaplain corps ministry. Not only does the military chaplain have to be physically fit and maintain a high level of physical fitness throughout his/her career, he will often serve in dangerous environments both in peacetime and in war. Where the troops are deployed, so goes the chaplain. Where they sleep, he sleeps. What they eat, he eats. All the comforts of home cannot be packed into his/her sea bag when deployed.

The chaplain is a non-combatant. He doesn't fire a weapon in a war zone nor kick in doors on a patrol but he/she does take care of the wounded and deals with the carnage of war. And the carnage can be great. Truth be told very few civilian parish pastors would survive on active duty. The military chaplain has not "left the ministry" running away from parish ministry to be a chaplain—as some in the church would assert—rather, the chaplain is engaging in ministry at the highest and most intense level to bring the Gospel of Christ Jesus to our men and women in uniform wherever they are stationed or deployed, in peace and in war, in the prime of their life and often in the most vulnerable days of their lives.

When I and my family arrived at Guardian Lutheran church in the summer of 1988, it was a small Lutheran church with a few families. Sunday morning worship attendance gathered approximately 30 souls. The church was located about one block off the beaten path from San Jose Boulevard. Just far enough not to be seen from the main highway, kind of hiding behind the Village Inn restaurant on the corner.

Guardian Lutheran was subsidized at that time by the Florida-Georgia district to the tune of about $2500 per month in order to pay the bills and keep the ministry viable. I was installed as the Pastor in July of 1988 and served as Guardian's pastor for the next six years. I also maintained an active status in the Naval Reserve which meant monthly drills for pay (2 days per month) and a two week commitment to train with my unit annually called ACDUTRA (Active Duty for Training) usually commencing in the summer.

The members of Guardian were a fine group of close-knit Lutheran saints who were eager to see Guardian grow and so was I. If this was the next footstep the Lord had laid out for me, then I must move forward, not look back but labor intensively in the present vineyard.[84]

Claude and Pat were our first contacts at the church. Claude was a generous and outstanding Christian gentleman whom I will never forget and Pat, a most gracious hostess. They provided us free lodging in their apartment complex on the Timuquana river our first year at Guardian while we were having our new house built in Mandarin. Claude was a combat Marine, Officer Corps, who served in the Korean war during some of the war's most difficult firefights against the Chinese and the North Korean communists. He received the Purple Heart from critical injuries sustained after a grenade blast. After the war he became financially successful in the real estate business and was the first millionaire I ever knew personally in my life. He was a well-respected pillar in the life of the church and has now passed on to his eternal reward.

The girls were 9, 7 and 4 years old in 1988. They made friends easily with the other kids at church and in our home neighborhood. Every Sunday morning, Connie would pack the van full with not only our kids but the neighborhood kids as well. Connie was never late for church or Sunday school. Guardian grew rapidly in those initial years.

Average church attendance went from 30 on a Sunday morning to 200 in three years. At the end of three years we were off District subsidy. One measure of our success was not only our members inviting their neighbors to church but as Pastor Bertram had taught me so well as his vicar the indispensable quality of wearing out the soles of your shoes in pursuit of souls for Christ. As a consequence, I stuck religiously to a plan to personally visit anyone in their home within two weeks after they had been a guest at our worship services on a previous Sunday. Simple but powerfully effective. Shoe soles pursuing lost souls

---

[84] Ecclesiastes is one of my favorite books of the Bible. Often I have preached from it, often I have drawn consolation and wisdom from Solomon's no-nonsense approach to this vain short life we live out under God's sun. My work ethic is taken from Ecclesiastes, "Whatever your hand finds to do, do it with all your might, for there is no work or device or knowledge or wisdom in the grave where you are going." Eccl. 9:10. Some might think that verse to be morbid. I find it exhilarating. *Carpe diem!* And while you're seizing the day by hard work do not let the joy of this hour be stolen by past regrets.

for Christ. During the home visit, I would present the Gospel, invite them back to church, and seek a commitment to join my new members class of several weeks in preparation for full church membership. It worked well, exceedingly well, and Guardian grew quickly with the Lord's blessing.

Our saints were young and energetic. Creative ministry events multiplied and the church sanctuary was renovated and enlarged to accommodate the growth. A pre-school was started and real plans were bandied about to start an elementary school on the back acreage of the church property. About a dozen of the girls of our good saints, ages eight to thirteen, were led and formed into a liturgical dance team which uniquely enhanced Sunday morning worship services at Guardian. It was a graceful and powerful witness to the Gospel of our Lord.

In addition, we held special veteran services for the community. During Desert Storm, the sanctuary was piled high with at least 50 large boxes of "goodies" given by the good saints that were sent to the troops overseas.

Guardian also had a few wonderful German-born native speakers in the congregation so it was natural to celebrate Oktoberfest every year and invite the community. Our choir was ably supported by Hazel our organist for a small but growing congregation. We all sang loud every Sunday, very loud.

During a Sunday congregational meeting attended by Rev. Dr. Tom Zehnder, the Florida-Georgia District President at that time, he announced that Guardian Lutheran was officially removed from the District's financial subsidy rolls. He then said, "I want you to know that Guardian Lutheran Church is the fastest growing church in the entire district." That was quite a compliment coming from your own District President considering that the congregation was being compared to more than 150 other congregations in the district. Guardian in its ministry history had never known such growth in three short years.

These were good years in the parish ministry and I was becoming more and more accustomed to the new mission God laid before me. I had been catapulted off the flight deck of His grace into a new world of parish ministry, saints of character, dancing children and expansive dreams.

The military is built around the chain of command from the top down and competence from the ground up. It doesn't quite work that way in the church. Strongly held opinions, various and sundry visions, inflexibility and human stubbornness vie for positions on a rotating Lazy Susan platter of church ideas. All are convinced they know exactly how the church should advance the mission of God. Often, competing ideas from pillars in the church can produce tension and checkmate other competing visions so that no one vision is pursued, the status quo becomes the fallback position and the saints are left treading water. The pastor's vision is just another point of view to consider. How much weight the pastor's vision carries is in the eye and the esteem of the beholder.

Swift numerical growth in any congregation, although a blessing, creates problems all its own. New talent and new ideas can be seen as threats and not blessings. The changing of the guard is not easy. The old guard isn't quite sure of the new guard nor does the old guard want to give up any position of authority or power in the church to the new guard. One would think that especially in the church of God reasonableness, love, humility and forgiveness would prevail but the sad truth is that even the redeemed saints of God created anew in the image of Christ Jesus can still act like a bunch of lousy sinners. The pastor is no exception. Therefore, the pastor and the congregation must take heed to the warning that when Judgment Day dawns, the righteous, according to the words of St. Peter, will "*scarcely* be saved."[85] Not much of a compliment, would you say? Nevertheless, Scripture speaks the unvarnished truth.

Small Bible study groups had been meeting in member's homes for

---

85   I Peter 4:18. "If the righteous one is *scarcely* saved, where will the ungodly and sinner appear?" Scarcely, in the sense of "hardly, with great difficulty" shall the righteous be saved. . . *ain't* that the truth!

a few months without the presence or leadership of the Pastor. By the Spring of 1993 during a congregational meeting, the plan was revealed that certain members of the Guardian Lutheran family wanted to break away and form a sister congregation on new real estate nearby. I came to the conclusion that such a competing vision of our future would not only damage future growth for the present church but would create a state of perpetual tension between Guardian and the new proposed "sister" congregation. If correct, I concluded that after all the hard work done to place Guardian back on the map, Guardian had most likely reached its growth ceiling and future ministry plans would stagnate in its present location.

Following that congregational meeting, the tremendous growth spurt at Guardian began to taper off. Worship attendance dwindled to 100 per week and then settled in around 50. These were trying and difficult days in the ministry, yet the grace of God is always greater than our sin and any present circumstance. A significant number of compassionate saints stayed in full support of their pastor and his family.

At the beginning of the sixth year of parish ministry, I knew I needed a break. I resigned my call in the summer of 1994 as the pastor of Guardian Lutheran church which placed me on CRM status within the District.[86]

What future ministry lay in store for me? Would there be more footsteps as God had promised through my baptism into Christ? Was there really a Divine plan and a design to the Christian's life in the midst of all this madness? What was God really doing in the lives of His saints? I was the circuit counselor[87] for all the LCMS congregations of the greater Jacksonville area during my years as pastor of Guardian Lutheran church. I had presided over the break-up of another congregation due

---

86   CRM: an ecclesiastical acronym meaning, Candidate for Reverend Ministry; that is, available and qualified to receive a pastoral call even though the candidate is not serving a congregation at the present time.

87   The role of circuit counselor was to organize regular circuit meetings, the agenda and speakers for local congregations in the circuit. The circuit counselor was also the official conduit between the District President, the local pastors and their congregations on official church matters.

to internal disputes. It wasn't pretty and I wished to spare the saints at Guardian the same pain.

Now that I had resigned temporarily from parish ministry, how would I provide for my wife and family? I had always believed that the gifts and calling of God into the ministry are irrevocable. Had not God chosen me to be a pastor early in life? Wasn't this His inescapable chosen vocation for me? Where were His footsteps now? Who would rescue me? Questions, questions, questions. God's unusual and gracious answer remained just beyond my ken but would soon arrive, and as always, just in time.

German to the Rescue

Ach, du Lieber! Genau zur rechten Zeit![88]

In the midst of all this turmoil at Guardian another footstep from God began to form before me quite unexpectedly. Mandarin High School, where Mandy attended, offered German. I soon launched a campaign to persuade Amanda, my oldest daughter, to sign up for German. Why German and not Spanish or some other language? Well, the answer was obvious. After all, I had taken a couple of years of German in High School myself, our Lutheran background was German, our last name was definitely German, Grandma Essig spoke German (whom Amanda was named after) and I would be able to help her ace the class! With these multiple cogent convincing arguments and sure-fire motivations, Mandy, with some fear and trepidation, signed up for German class much to my delight. Now, whether or not she agreed to this out of love for her father or an easy way to get an A in class, was never divulged.

---

88   German: Oh my goodness! Just at the right time!

GERMAN TO THE RESCUE

When Mandy started German in the Fall of 1993, her teacher abruptly resigned at the end of September for reasons unknown. Following her resignation a number of substitute teachers were paraded before the class, all of whom knew no German. This infuriated me. How could Mandy learn *Die Muttersprache*[89] accurately if the subs knew little or no German at all? *Das ist einfach Verrückt!*[90] The solution? Dad to the rescue.

Shortly after this teaching famine for German knowledge was revealed to me, I went over and presented myself and my academic credentials to the principal persuading him that I should be his next German teacher. I don't know whether he was desperate for a teacher-solution or whether I had convinced him that I could handle the job, but I was hired on the spot. He was delighted at my offer. God's new footstep was beginning to take shape right before my eyes. There is no end to baptismal grace in this earthly life.

Without spilling the beans to Mandy that I was hired to be her new German teacher, the next morning I simply entered my assigned German classroom and waited for the students to arrive. Mandy's shocked look as she walked through the door and saw her Dad at the teacher's desk was classic and unforgettable. Her jaw dropped, her eyes popped, she smiled nervously and took her seat. Of course, I kept the father-daughter relationship in the class room mum for as long as I could but eventually the word leaked out. Yes, Mandy did survive and marvelously passed the German class.

For the next two years father and daughter journeyed through *Das Vaterland*[91] together. In the classroom as her father relentlessly interrogated her fellow students on German grammar, she knew she could not fake her studies. I believe I can say, without undue bias, I'm proud of the fact that as her father/teacher/tutor she managed to ace German all the way through, but I'm afraid that if you ask Mandy to speak any

---

89   German: The mother tongue, The native language.
90   German: That's just crazy!
91   German: The Fatherland.

German today, all you will probably hear is, *"Nein, Nein!"*

I love languages and language study. I've engaged in countless hours pursuing competency in Biblical Hebrew, NT Greek[92], German, Latin and a smattering of Arabic and Ugarit. Now with a new opportunity arising, namely, a more detailed and committed study of the German language, I believed I owed it to my students and myself to pursue excellence so I applied and was accepted into the MA German program in the summer of 1994 at the University of Florida, Gainesville. The commitment to study German at this level for the next six years (1994-1999) refocused my mind away from the troubles at Guardian during my last year as the church's pastor. New footsteps, new script. New direction. God is not only good, He's highly creative!

Acquiring fluency in any foreign language in middle age is difficult. It's easier to learn the sounds and grammar intuitively in elementary school years when the mind is so supple and more receptive than as an adult. As an adult second language learner, the learner is acutely aware and frequently embarrassed by their accent or lack thereof. Initial attempts to speak German correctly can often be laughable or ridiculed by insensitive native speakers. The best course of action is to move to the target country and become immersed in the language and culture for at least six months. That would be *Wunderbar!* But such an opportunity and the attendant cost was not an option to me.

Nevertheless, no sooner had I matriculated at UF in the German MA program than I found myself in the middle of Germany during the summer of 1994 with a dozen other German high school teachers at various levels of German proficiency in the MA program. The summer program in *Deutschland* consisted of one month of classroom

---

92   The word of Scripture embedded in New Testament Greek has opened my eyes to remarkable insights into the Word of God. Not only are the very words of God inspired and God-breathed but also the very grammar of the language through which God has chosen to reveal Himself to His world. My NT Greek professor at the seminary, Dr. Buls, use to tell his students, "Pay attention to the tenses in Greek! There are sermons in the Greek tenses!" I believed him then and still do now. Greek is a precise language revealing God's intended sense in a way few other languages on earth are capable. In so doing God makes clear the meaning of His script for our life and the details of His footsteps for our days.

learning and cultural acquaintance. It was a thrilling, exciting and a apprehensive challenge for me while in Germany where every voice heard and every sign read seemed scrambled, foggy and a real impediment to my learning curve in the German language. For me at the time, even the simplest urgent question like, "Where's the bathroom?" took far too long to formulate on the tip of my tongue before an accident might materialize! Culture shock is a real phenomenon. But my professors assured me there is no better way to learn the German language. I agreed but one month wasn't going to cut it.

Professor Franz Futterknecht, the director of the MA German program at UF, took a liking to his new student. He was well aware of my church background and pleased that a son of the Lutheran church was studying Luther's language in depth. When he assigned housing for his students in Germany that summer, he housed me with his uncle, Mr. Herbert Bader, a fine gentleman who knew no English. I was just at the beginning of my resurrection of German. Professor Futterknecht thought the arrangement would force the German language out of my lips more quickly. Between Herbert and myself, our attempted communications led to some hilarious exchanges.

During the summer of 1994 Germany was playing the USA in the FIFA world cup of soccer. We parked ourselves in front of the TV in his apartment and watched the game. Herbert opened a fine bottle of wine with two glasses. As the game commenced and after a couple of glasses of wine, the fruit of the vine began to add a growing boldness and confidence to my tongue. I was eager to speak something, anything, to my gracious host in German. Courageously, I pieced together the following sentence and when I was confident that he, Mr. Herbert Bader, would actually understand my conversation I took another gulp of wine and began the dialogue. I asked him:

"Bitte, Herbert, Sag mir, warum denkst du denn die Deutschen den Zweite Weltkrieg begonnen haben?"

Now you would think that anyone with half a brain thousands of miles from home and a guest in a stranger's house in the middle of Germany would have more sense that to ask your gracious host, "Mr. Bader, so please tell me, why do you think the Germans began World War II?"

He wasn't offended, although he should have been, instead he rose instantly from his chair, stood erect, and turned toward me. I had enough sense to perceive from the obvious cultural clues that I should rise to the occasion, and I did. I arose from my seat. Herbert towered over me by a foot. He looked down at me sternly and offered a one word answer, "Stolz, Herr Schreiber, Stolz!!"

Wow! Great answer! I had no idea what he had just said but was confident that a break-through in international relationships had just been renewed between our native countries. I had asked a question in German that I thought would be a real conversation starter, a simple, innocent question in fledgling German. He understood me and answered me. Fluency in German had just begun. *Ausgezeichnet!*[93]

But I wasn't quite certain of his answer. It was a short conversation. What the heck is "Stolz" anyway? Sounds like the name of a new German beer. We both sat down and immediately I ran to my German-English dictionary for the answer. Over the years, I have pondered his answer from many angles. "Pride, Mr. Schreiber, pride!" that was Herbert's answer to the origin of World War II. Amazing. Insightful. Trenchant. Frank. Powerful.

Learning another tongue besides your own, opens the mind to a brand new worldview, at the same time enlarging your own mental horizons, empathy and understanding. By the grace of God at just the right time, German had come to the rescue and saved me by reorienting me toward a new world of academia and teaching which led me to read and translate Luther's German Bible in Fraktur type and engage other theological writings of the early Lutheran church fathers. There

---

93   German: Excellent!

was work to be done, great work indeed. Moreover, the footsteps of God had not left me nor had His script for my life ended. The past months of bitterness, anger and turmoil were quickly receding replaced by new learning adventures, new friends and new teaching opportunities in the new footsteps of God. "Behold, I am making all things new!" Rev. 21:5. Yes, dear God, you are. A new mission from the bow of His flight deck had been launched.

Public High School Teacher—Full Time

"Don't get too comfortable."[94]

Whoever first said that work is therapy was right. The flip side of that proverbial coin is also correct, "An idle brain is the devil's workshop."[95] The purpose of CRM status within our church body is to rejuvenate, to reorient and to reinvigorate one's ministry with new perspectives and new horizons. It is not meant to be a time to loaf, play golf, soak up TV, catch up on FB, get lazy, get fat or be idle.

The summer after teaching HS German part-time was followed by the opportunity to teach full-time at Mandarin Senior High School beginning in the Fall of 1994. It was a new horizon and an invigorating possibility. Apparently, the Principal was satisfied enough that German had been saved in the curriculum from extinction. He now offered me a new challenge.

"How's your Latin, Herr Schreiber?" Well, I had always loved Latin and successfully completed two years of Latin in high school. It wasn't

---

[94] Brain to self (or was it the Holy Spirit in a still small voice?) speaking to me in the midst of a brief full-time public high school teaching career.
[95] This proverb has many incarnations with its roots in Scripture: "Laziness casts one into a deep sleep, and an idle person will suffer hunger." Proverbs 19:15. And again, "Because of laziness the building decays, and through idleness of hands the house leaks." Ecclesiastes 10:18. The Living Bible paraphrases Proverbs 16:27, "Idle hands are the Devil's workshop, idle lips are his mouthpiece."

my major but in fact, in my second year of Latin I was placed in an honors Latin class separate from the main group. Good for me. But, teach Latin today? At that point in my life, Latin was 30 years in my rear view mirror.

"Sure! Good to go!" I responded with little hesitation. Whether I agreed out of a swelled ego, a puffed up head or financial desperation, it was the latter that took precedence. We needed the money, like, right now.

Going CRM status with the District meant no income from the parish ministry. In order to pay the bills and stay afloat, Connie and I had to find income immediately. Connie was soon hired full-time to serve as a Paraprofessional with special-needs children at Mandarin Oaks Elementary School, a most difficult and compassionate work which she continued to do for the next ten years.[96] In the Fall of 1994 I took the reins of my new position as the new full-time teacher of German, Latin and Psychology (my undergraduate college major) at Mandarin Senior High School, Jacksonville, Florida.

God knew what he was doing. Work, hard work is therapy. My learning curve was steep. German was coming along well but I had to resurrect Latin quickly. (I barely kept a chapter ahead of my Latin students). Psychology was a much easier road to travel. All of this head work kept my mind off past church tensions, past gripes, complaints and bickering so much so that I began to love the give and take of the classroom. Engaging young minds in the pursuit of knowledge with banter and challenge in their teenage years kept me lively on my feet and quick with my wits. Perhaps, I thought, I was cut out to be a German language teacher and a Latin scholar for the rest of my life. What new and exciting discoveries in the world of scholarship would

---

[96] Connie at the same time worked three years for the Duval county Sheriff's department as a school crossing guard at Mandarin Oaks. It was during this time in the school cafeteria that Connie saved a child's life from choking with the Heimlich maneuver. She was recognized and honored by the Sheriff's department in a special ceremony. Compassion is Connie's middle name.

this opportunity lead to?! I felt just like Professor Lindenbrook, a renowned geologist, played by James Mason in the 1959 blockbuster movie, "Journey to the Center of the Earth."[97] "The greatest discoveries are right under our feet!" he exclaimed. Indeed, great discoveries in the teaching profession now lie right under my nose and all I had to do was obtain the necessary professional credentials, degrees and competence. No problem. I always loved school anyway. God's footsteps were again clear and a new journey had begun. God's covenant to me in Baptism provided all the extraordinary grace I would need to accomplish the task.

Not so fast, not so fast! There's always a fly in the ointment, somewhere. In my case the "flies" appeared in the seventh period, Monday through Friday, in a peer counseling class that I was assigned to teach. Apparently, it was the class, that the faculty took turns teaching. It was the class from hell that the faculty loved to hate. The class was filled with about 30 high school students who for whatever reason were underperformers with an attitude, usually a bad attitude. Somehow the teacher was supposed to take charge of the unruly bunch of students and shepherd them through the delights of attitude adjustment fifty minutes a day, five days a week and emerge victorious at the end of the semester with 30 "born again" well-adjusted teenage academics.

It didn't quite work that way. I loved the first six periods of the day, but the seventh period, which ended my teaching day, I dreaded. It was much like the sitcom, "Welcome Back, Kotter," played by Gabe Kaplan but unlike the so-called "Sweat hogs" in the TV sitcom who were remedial with potential many of my seventh grade period students were intractable with a nasty edge.

---

[97] The movie is based on the book of the same title by Jules Verne. One of Professor Lindenbrook's star students, Alex (Pat Boone), gifts the professor with an unusually heavy volcanic rock within which is a hidden plumb bob. When the lava is melted away a cryptic inscription written in blood on the plumb bob is discovered. It is a message from a fellow scientist and geologist named Arne Saknussemm who 300 years earlier claimed to have found a passageway to the very center of the earth. The entry point, Saknussemm wrote on the plumb bob, was an extinct volcano in Iceland.

To be sure, I treated all fairly and gave it my best shot in the midst of the frequently heard F-bomb but I could claim little success and saw little progress. I'm sure it was God's way of saying, "Don't get too comfortable in this footstep. I know you love to teach and I made you that way but this is only a pause on the highway back to Gospel ministry." A still small voice in the back of my head kept saying, "The gifts and the calling of God into His Gospel ministry are irrevocable." Romans 11:29. Absolutely true.

Nevertheless, the Lord can call His disciples away at any time to rest for a little while from the business and incessant needs of the world clamoring for our attention.[98] This footstep, though filled with busy academic work, grading papers, teaching and studying was just a pause from the pastoral vocation. I knew in my heart of hearts what God had called me to do in His kingdom and that would never change.

Timing is everything in life. God's timing is perfect and always right on time. It is the first thing we need to know and learn when seeking the footsteps of God's mission for our life. Here comes the Lord, once again, with His extraordinary grace for just another ordinary life. It is a script I could never have written out of my own wits. Thank God. Roger that.

Chewed Out

"Mea culpa, mea culpa, mea maxima culpa."[99]

It is rare for a chaplain to ever get chewed out by a superior officer in the performance of his military duties. Admonished, maybe, but chewed out? Therefore, I can announce to you, my dear reader, that I

---

98 Mark 6:31. "And He said to them, "Come aside by yourselves, to a deserted place and rest a while."
99 Latin: "My fault, my own fault, my own most grievous fault." A confession of ultimate remorse and the personal acceptance of full blame as charged.

CHEWED OUT

hold the rare distinction and privilege of having being chewed out and dressed down not once but twice in my career. Of course, from my side of the story, there is plenty of room for self-justification but to be honest, I'll have to admit there is some truth on their side of the story as well.

The first incident occurred early in my career while driving on base at Marine Corps Air Station, Jacksonville, North Carolina. The year was 1983. I had one year of active duty under my belt and feeling great. Driving down the main drag just past the Air Station chapel, I was pulled over by the base police for no apparent reason. I was given a speeding ticket for doing 30 mph in a 25 mph zone. Whoopie-do. That's what I thought until I appeared before the Provost Marshall at the base station police department.

The Marine Major in charge, one rank my superior, locked my heels in front of his desk and called me to attention while he read the riot act to me about base protocol and driving privileges. Before he was through, he tossed in a few choice words about how as an officer and especially a Chaplain, I should be setting the example for all enlisted personnel. I thought the whole confrontation was overkill but the Major wasn't laughing. It did cure me of one thing. After that day I never exceeded the base speed limits again, not even by a single mile per hour.

The second incident occurred many years later, about 14 to be exact. I was still very active in the Naval Reserve throughout the nineties while serving as a parish pastor. My unit drilled monthly on the weekend at Naval Air Station, Jacksonville, Florida. Mandatory all hands formation occurred promptly at 0730 on the parade deck. If you were late, for whatever reason, it would be duly noted in your record.

Yes, I was late for formation one Saturday morning, but barely late. After my unit had already formed and were standing at attention waiting for colors to be played, I thought I spied an opportunity to sneak into line from the back without the CO noticing me. I did and it appeared he didn't. However, about thirty minutes later when all hands were inside the building and busy at their desks I was called away to the CO's office. I had no real clue why he wanted to see me.

I went upstairs and strolled into his office. He saw me, called me to attention, locked my heels beside his desk and read me the riot act for a number of protocols I had broken without his permission. The main issue appeared to be my absence during Sunday morning drills because at the time I was the sole pastor of Redeemer Lutheran Church, Lake City, Florida, and unable to leave the pulpit unattended once a month. For chaplains serving in the Naval Reserves, it was usually assumed that if he was the sole pastor of a congregation, his Sunday morning drill time could be performed at a different time during the week at the Reserve center. Devastating key word: Assume! Without the CO's explicit approval in writing the Chaplain is supposed to be with his unit on Sunday morning and nowhere else. I had assumed a prerogative that wasn't mine to assume.

I stood at rigid attention while the strident gravel voice of my CO raged in my ears, raised my blood pressure and flushed my face red. When he was through, I realized that it was my fault, my own fault, my own most grievous fault, as Lutherans like to confess liturgically. My rank was Commander. My Commanding Officer was a Captain, one rank higher, but both ranks are considered to be senior officers in the Navy. Yes, it was a royal smack-down. My flip attitude at the time which had been encrusted over with a veneer of arrogance was being "reframed" military style, to borrow a word from the world of VA contemporary psychological counseling.

Seeing that a Chaplain's FITREP must be signed off by his/her commanding officer before it is put in the officer's permanent official record, where it would remain until the next promotion board, I knew I would take a hit, probably a major hit. The competition to make Captain in the Navy—for most officers the pinnacle in their twenty year career—had just been jettisoned off the flight deck of my career into the deep blue sea. Eagle wings and a fourth stripe would never be seen on my uniform, so I believed.

It was 1997. I was less than three years from finishing a twenty year career and picking up a retirement check for life but at the moment, I was despondent and fatigued with the Navy and I came within a whisker of resigning my commission altogether. Fervent prayers for guidance were launched heavenward but no sure answers descended. God's footsteps had seem to evaporate into thin air. His script for my life vanished like disappearing ink on white paper. Not knowing why and without strong convictions, I decided to try and stick it out for a while and persevere as unpleasant as I knew it would be under the current CO of my Reserve unit and the new female CO that would soon follow him. My loose ends were unraveling and fluttering in the afternoon breeze which dusted over the footprints of God making them indistinct and indistinguishable to read. Any celestial guidance that might be launched from on high was impossible to discern. No footprints, no script. No script, no mission. No mission, no launch. No launch and I'm just screwed waiting to be tossed over the side of the ship to make room for the next plane.

One Loose Screw Secured

Das ist alles. . . alles ist fertig.[100]

"Hope springs eternal in the human breast. Man never *is*, but always *to be* blest."[101] or so we all want to believe. There was one hopeful loose end that was tied down during these days; namely, the completion of my Doctor of Ministry degree. In 1991, I had started a Doctor

---

100 German: That's everything! Everything is ready (done).
101 Charles Eliot, ed. *The Harvard Classics*. English Poetry: Vol 40. (New York: P.F. Collier & Son Company, 1910), 410. Alexander Pope, English poet of the Enlightenment (1688-1744). From "An Essay on Man.".

of Ministry degree program at Faith Evangelical Lutheran Seminary, Tacoma, Washington. My dissertation focused on resurrecting the office of the evangelist in the life of the church, a topic I was convinced needed diligent attention and a fresh new approach considering the dwindling numbers of Lutheran church-goers in the United States and most main-line denominations. Work is good therapy. Healthy for mind and body. This footstep seem to have God's full support and it did. "The end of a work is always much better than its beginning," opined Solomon the Wise (Eccl. 7:8). I wholeheartedly agree.

I "took the walk," along with my graduating class, June 15, 1996. The graduation ceremony was held in Central Lutheran Church, Tacoma, Washington whose pastor, Rev. Dr. Reuben H. Redal had founded Faith Evangelical Seminary in 1969. Dr. Redal served as the Seminary president until his sudden death in 2006 at the age of 85. This loose-end footstep had been secured; a new script from God would soon be engaged.

8th Marine Corps Recruiting District

Carpe Diem!
"For the night is coming when no one can work."
John 9:4[102]

Although the entire chaplain corps in the late 90s was comprised of about 3,000 chaplains, I never had the pleasure of knowing or working with Chaplain Jack Lea, Captain, US Navy. The desire to return to active duty even at this late date in my military career was just as strong as ever, should the opportunity present itself.

---

102   Latin: "Seize the day!" In other words, grab the opportunity, it may not pass by this way again which is parallel in thought to what Christ Jesus has said, "I must work the works of Him who sent Me while it is day; for the night is coming when no one can work." John 9:4

Chaplain Lea had just received orders to serve with Marine Corps Recruiting Command, Headquarters, Quantico, Virginia. Shortly thereafter, he had persuaded the General of the need for chaplains to serve with each recruiting command, of which there were six, geographically spread across the nation. Never before in the history of the Corps, had chaplains been assigned to serve with Marine Corps recruiters. Chaplain Lea's vision was dependent upon the success of the first chaplain to be assigned. Jack promulgated the word officially throughout the Chaplain Corps defining the parameters necessary for any reserve chaplain interested to serve for six months of active duty with MCRD. He then initiated the search for the right chaplain beginning with a series of chaplain interviews in the Fall of 1999. I leaped at the opportunity and put my best foot forward in uniform.

The world of Marine Corps recruiting is a very high stress billet, second only to combat as many Marine recruiters liked to say. The reason? Every Marine Corps recruiter is selected from the best of the best to be a recruiter because of his/her "poster-boy Marine Corps" appearance and qualities. Each new recruiter following recruiter training has to prove their mettle by rolling in two new recruits into the Marine Corps from the nation's public high schools every month for the duration of their three year set of orders. To do less than two recruits per month was a hit on his/her stellar record. Repeat performances of failing to recruit two recruits per month would quickly ruin your chances for promotion. The average work-week was long and hard (60 plus hours), the travel incessant and the recruits could be fickle and unreliable regarding initial appointments. Depending upon the adaptability of the recruiter to a sales-oriented job from his previous MOS[103] and his/her learning curve potential, the tour could turn out to be a stellar career enhancing personal growth opportunity of a lifetime, or it could turn out to be the tour from hell.[104]

---

103 MOS: Military Occupation Specialty
104 There were a number of suicidal incidents related to the extreme stress of Marine Corps recruiting duty during the four years I served as District Chaplain, 8th MCRD, New Orleans,

What can a Chaplain do to relieve the stresses inherent in Marine Corps recruiting? It all depends upon the chaplain. Marriages take a big hit during a tour with Marine Corps Recruiting Command because of the long work hours and lack of time with the family. If the chaplain has expertise in leading marriage workshops, he can alleviate a lot of stress by keeping couples talking to each other, and navigate through work and family tensions ever present during the recruiter's tour of duty. If the chaplain has expertise in the world of salesmanship, he can teach and brief the recruiters on the art of salesmanship via the lens of learned optimism in approaching a potential recruit. If the chaplain understands the educational world he can open new doors for the recruiter into the world of private Christian schools as a regular base for recruitment into the Marine Corps.

In the Fall of 1999 while serving as Pastor of Redeemer Lutheran Church, Lake City, Florida, I was interviewed by Chaplain Lea and selected unhesitatingly for the new billet. Orders quickly followed to serve on active duty with the 8th Marine Corps Recruiting District headquartered in New Orleans. The new orders were written initially for six months but I would soon discover that grand success was written all over this new footprint from God. Not only was I able to offer multiple workshops on marriage, teach learned optimism as a salesmanship skill but I was also able to open multiple private Christian schools to the world of Marine Corps recruiting which option had rarely if ever been tested before. Whatever eased the burden for recruiters to engage and recruit quality candidates to serve as future Marines was not only greatly appreciated by Command and the individual Marine Corps recruiters, it exponentially multiplied the chances that the newly designated chaplain billet would survive, prosper and spread

---

2000-2004. One particular recruiter, a Staff Sergeant in the Marine Corps and hand-picked for recruiting duty completed suicide leaving a hand-written note damning the Corps for his failure to roll two recruits into the Corps every month despite Marine Corps remedial training. Salesmanship skills are difficult to learn and for some Marines, nearly impossible. I performed his memorial service at his home town in Waco, Texas. Surely, there was a better God-given script for this Marine and his family instead of suicide.

8TH MARINE CORPS RECRUITING DISTRICT

to the other five recruiting districts as well, and it did. My initial set of orders to New Orleans metamorphosized into four years of active duty with the 8th Marine Corps Recruiting Command.[105] One ordinary life was touched once again by extraordinary grace. God's baptismal grace had never left me. Never did I think in my wildest dreams that I would have another opportunity to serve on active duty but God blessed my restless heart with a unique, challenging golden footprint to serve with the Marines once again.

Chaplain Williams to my left became the District Chaplain for the 6th Marine Corps Recruiting District in Kansas City, 2002. Colonel Parkhurst, USMC, to my immediate right was the CO of the 8th MCRD, New Orleans, when I arrived in 2000. Chaplain Jack Lea, far right, was the Command Chaplain for MCRC in Quantico, Virginia and initiated the vision and need for chaplains to serve with Marine Corps recruiters.

---

105 Chaplain Schreiber was recalled to active duty from January 2000 to January 2004, where he served in a newly designated billet as District Chaplain for the 8th Marine Corps Recruiting District, New Orleans, ministering to 900 Marine recruiters and their families dispersed over a ten-state area in the Midwest. During the same period of time, Chaplain Schreiber graduated from the Marine Corps Command and Staff College, June 2003.

Evangelism—Marine Corps Style

Be harmless as doves but sly as a fox.[106]

I love Marines. I love the way they attack and succeed in their mission, no matter what. I love their professionalism, their incessant striving for excellence and their Rocky-like attitude toward life. I love their humor which can be caustic, biting and brutally honest but still hilarious. A thin-skinned chaplain serving with Marines won't last long; on the other hand, a thick-skinned chaplain can't help but pick up some of their finer traits (!)

Amanda, our eldest daughter, tried out for an American professional football cheerleadering team in 2000. She made the first cut and every cut thereafter for the next six years. Few women can claim such fame. I was one proud papa together with one proud mama. It quickly became rumored shortly after I arrived at New Orleans that one of the chaplain's daughters was a professional football cheerleader. (Of course, I did nothing to squelch the rumor and everything to promote it.) Understanding the Marine mentality to always look twice at a pretty girl, the revelation came to me that professional football cheerleaders might be a ticket to real evangelism among these recruiters.

My technique was simple. Behind my office door on the wall I had posted a large, full-color unsigned poster of an entire American professional football cheerleading squad. Naturally, once the word got out, every Marine in the building had to investigate and investigate they did. Whenever a Marine would stroll into my office and say, "Hey Chap, I heard that your daughter is a professional football cheerleader. Is that really true?!" My response was always the same.

---

[106] Matthew 10:16. The text literally reads, "Be wise as serpents and harmless as doves." Seems to me there is an easy correlation between the "wise" strategy of the serpent in the Garden of Eden who deceived our first parents and thereby the entire world and the Devil's meandering, serpentine, sly as a fox, entry into the human heart.

EVANGELISM—MARINE CORPS STYLE

I would usher the Marine into my office and direct his attention to the large poster of pretty girls in their cheerleading uniforms on the wall. After sufficient gazing and drooling, the Marine would ask, "So which one, Chap, is your daughter?" That was my cue to walk over to the door and close it quietly behind the unsuspecting Marine. With his eyes still glued to the poster, I would engage in light-hearted flippant conversation but never point out to the Marine which one of the beauties was Amanda which just kept him guessing and pointing to various cheerleaders while I kept nodding a definite maybe. When the gazing and drooling was done, and the office door closed, I offered him a seat at which time I would engage in a little light conversation, mixed with a little God-talk while navigating the tête-à-tête toward the Gospel and the real truths in life that matter. Worked for me. Worked for God, And most importantly, it often worked for the Marine. I call it "sly as a fox" evangelism.

Our daughter Amanda, an All-American professional football cheerleader.

Divine Linkage

"The Word of God cannot be broken."
John 10:35[107]

When I checked aboard 8th MCRD, New Orleans, in mid-January, 2000, it was an unusual frosty day for the Crescent City. That day began what turned out to be four more years of active duty. I was in-zone that fiscal year before the board to be considered for promotion to the rank of Captain, 06. I failed to select. I was not surprised. After the chewing-out debacle with my CO at my last Reserve duty station at NAS, JAX, my FITREP record was not sufficiently competitive compared to my fellow chaplains to earn the promotion. The promotion rate for chaplains in-zone from Commander 05 to Captain 06 is approximately 50% but can vary depending upon a variety of limiting factors. Above-zone chaplains will still be looked at each FY until their retirement but their chances of selection drop to single digits after the first non-select and grow progressively worse every non-select thereafter. Nevertheless, I proceeded with hope that hard work, perseverance and trusting God's script might have a chance of success sometime in the future, even if slim.

In addition to the typical chaplain duties of crisis counseling, memorial services, invocations and guest preaching, I also presented numerous PPT briefs at Recruiting stations on a wide variety of relevant topics related to salesmanship in the recruiting effort. I conducted

---

[107] Scripture cannot be broken. The Greek NT reads: ου δυναται λυθηναι η γραφη. λυθηναι is an aorist passive infinitive. In other words, "Scripture is not able to be broken." The passive voice of the infinitive demands an agent and an answer for our faith. Who or what is able to break the Word of God? Answer? No one, and not one thing. This assertion covers the entire corpus of the very Word of God, all of its precious promises culminating and centered in Christ Jesus, the Lord and Savior of the world. This text certainly includes God's script for your earthly life which He has prepared, written and delivered for your salvation and all the works of your sanctified Christian life. Ponder again the meaning of Ephesians 2:10 as stated in the Epigraph of this book. Your life will flow exactly as written in the script of God.

multiple marriage workshops on station and set up a nation-wide network of Reserve Chaplains in support of Marine Corps Recruiting Command for all Districts.

But the single item that pleased me most and gained the greatest respect from the Marine recruiters is that I would accompany the recruiter to the individual high schools in his area helping him/her to gain/improve access for recruiting purposes. Once inside the front doors of the high school with the recruiter my first step was to set up a friendly chat with the principal.

Over 80 high schools located in ten states were visited during my four years at New Orleans. The schools were both public and private. Rapport and recruiter access was established in many cases where none previously existed. Before my tour, recruiters had largely bypassed the private Christian school market as unapproachable or less than fruitful, however, a Chaplain in uniform with the cross on his lapel gained instant rapport the moment he walked through the door side by side with the Marine recruiter and spoke to the office staff, saying, "May I speak with the principal?"

I learned a great lesson about Gospel ministry at New Orleans. Simply this. Unless the chaplain makes his/her ministry truly relevant to the unique real needs of the Command wherever he/she serves and earns their respect, any kind of Christ-centered ministry in their midst will be difficult and bear little fruit. When the word went out that the chaplain was able to open up the private school market and was more than willing to join in with the recruiter's presentations before the full high school assembly at both public and private schools, thus making the mission of rolling two recruits into the Corps every month less stressful, well, all I can say is that it was wonderful to be so wanted and invited to speak so frequently throughout the 8th Marine Corps District. It was a grand four year tour indeed and a marvelous adventure, "Simply marvelous!"

You can imagine my jaw-dropping shock and suspender-busting

surprise when the results of the FY 03 Captain Staff Reserve Selection board were released and my name was on the list. Not only was this my third look above zone which put my chances for success barely negligible (I'm guessing about 25:1) but I was the only chaplain to be selected for promotion to Navy Captain that fiscal year.[108]

Why is it important to relate the details of my script to you apart from my own personal satisfaction? Because I seek to demonstrate clearly to you the divine linkage that your faith might be strengthened.

Here's the linkage. Without being recalled to active duty late in my Navy Chaplain career, there would have been no chance to be promoted to Captain. Without the promotion to Captain I could not be nominated nor apply to be the next endorsing agent of The Lutheran Church-Missouri Synod, which position just happened to become available as I concluded my fourth year at 8th MCRD, New Orleans, in 2004. The parameters for the church position designated that the nominee must hold the rank of 06, which is Captain if the nominee is Navy. Without being selected in the church's interview process against several well-qualified applicants, there would have been no opportunity to give back to the Chaplain Corps and especially the LCMS chaplains of my own church body, the joy of ministry in Christ that I had so richly experienced throughout my years. Divine linkage? Absolutely. How could this ordinary earthly life interpret this scenario any differently?

The good works that God has already prepared for all baptized believers into Christ Jesus are not just a disconnected series of haphazard footprints laid before us but a script of love, coherence and cohesion based upon the gracious gifts God has already placed into the believer's life in Christ since baptism. Ordinary lives made extraordinary by His present grace. To believe this is eternal comfort that calms the troubled soul.

---

108 See Appendix 4: Naval Reserve Promotions to the Grades of Captain, Commander, Lieutenant Commander, Lieutenant, Line and Staff Corps, and Warrant Officers. Dated 24 November 2003. After each officer's name selected for promotion are eight numbers; the first four are the last four numbers of the officer's SSN, after the slash mark are the four numbers of the Naval Officer's designator. The Chaplain Corps designator is 4100s. There was only one 4105 officer selected for promotion to Captain in the Chaplain Corps from the FY 2003 promotion board.

Therefore, to the baptized Christian reader I say, "Seek His script diligently! Pursue His footprints!" God's script won't float down to you from heaven as you lounge in your easy chair or be cryptically written on the side of your frothy beer mug. If you search the Word diligently, you will learn to see the Divine linkage between the events in your ordinary life. The linkage between all the crosses and all the joys of your life is Divine, real and for your good. God controls the script. He threads the eye of the needle and traps you safely upon His flight deck of grace.

What happened to me is equally available for you. My life is not so special. I am not the only one whom God loves nor does God need me to run His universe. Yet, He has surrounded my life by His gracious love in every circumstance, at every bolter across His flight deck, and in every time and place.

The many strands of rope called your earthly life, God weaves together and threads the eye of the needle pulling you through into the Kingdom of God. In this way His gracious script pulls your feet from the toes of one footstep to the heel of the next. All your days are divinely linked by the grace of God. This is a peace that surpasses all human understanding.

The New World of Endorsing Agent

The day that I checked aboard and first sat in my St. Louis office at Synod headquarters as the new endorsing agent was filled with thrilling expectations of the work to be done and anxiety about the new learning curve I immediately experienced. I was now the registered DOD endorsing agent[109] for the LCMS and the pastor to about 180

---

[109] Rank Has Its Privileges, RHIP. Everyone in DOD is ranked according to an assigned lineal precedence number from the Commander in Chief, who is ranked #1, down through all military ranks. Therefore, every military member can know exactly who is senior and junior within his/her own current rank and the broader ranking structure of the entire military

plus chaplains, their families and their ministries wherever they were stationed, worldwide. There had been a short turn-over file and brief with the outgoing endorsing agent, which was helpful, but his assistant had also retired at the same time leaving me with no other pair of ears to discuss strategy, mission and focus for our chaplains.

A fellow Navy chaplain and good friend, Chaplain Mark Steiner, Captain, US Navy, now retired, was a surprise gift from God. Because of his work in the Chief of Chaplains office as Deputy Executive Assistant (2000-2004) and SME[110] for the Department of Justice and the Navy Judge Advocate General on many legal matters of consequence to the Chaplain Corps, Steiner had a distinct handle and a current knowledge base of all the regulations and controversial issues with which I would need to be thoroughly familiar for all branches of the service as the endorsing agent. Shortly after coming on board, I remember distinctly the day when I cracked open a large box with my name on it and no return label, as I recall. I pulled out a big fat notebook (or was it two?) carefully wrapped and mailed from the Chief of Chaplain's office via the courtesy of Mark Steiner. This began my education for the position I would hold for the next ten years. Just knowing I had a helping hand in high places went a long way to relieving the stress of the first year on the job.

The spin cycle of life never ends. What once was, dawns again; what is to be will be traced out by today's footprints and then repeated in different garb by the next generation, but the essence and principles of life are repeated over and over and over again. So observed Solomon the Wise[111] and I believe him, except for just one little thing, the pro-

---

establishment. It use to be in previous regulations that the official endorsing agent of any denomination held the equivalent rank of a one star flag officer. This recognition supported enhanced protocols whenever the endorsing agent of any denomination would officially visit his/her chaplains stationed at any military bae. This ensured that the endorsing agent's lodging and official visit with the Command would be VIP comfortable. Another little perk supplied by the grace of God through the courtesy of Uncle Sam.

110   SME: Subject Matter Expert
111   Ecclesiastes 1: 9, 10. That which has been is what will be, that which is done is what will be done, and there is nothing new under the son. Is there anything of which it may be said, "See,

THE NEW WORLD OF ENDORSING AGENT

verbial fly in the ointment, it's still all new *to me* today.

Nancy Rowley, my Assistant to the Director, served God, church and country faithfully and professionally for my entire ten years of service. She was the corporate memory when I began which I desperately needed to understand in order to assimilate the cycle of new work ahead of me. My immediate boss was Rev. Dr. Robert Roegner, also new to his position but who gave me the freedom and support to engage in new initiatives for the good of the Chaplain Corps without the downward drag of micromanagement. Of absolute vital significance for their combined military knowledge, insight and wisdom was my MAF[112] committee through whom all candidates seeking endorsement would be vetted and interviewed prior to active or reserve duty. The MAF committee was my sounding board for all visions, plans and implementation of new ministry programs for our military, Civil Air Patrol and VA chaplains.

One year after I began my duties as Director, Chaplain LtCol Ted Wuerffel, USAF was called to be the Associate Director for MAF (2005-2008). One of the distinct highlights during his tenure was our joint collaboration with Concordia Historical Institute on the campus of Concordia Seminary, St. Louis. Under the direction and invitation of Dr. Martin Noland MAF was invited to advise, embellish and support a new chaplain corps exhibit.[113] The exhibit was magnificent. What was

---

this is new"? It has already been in ancient times before us.

112   MAF: For the ten years (2004-2014) that I served as Director, Ministry to the Armed Forces, I was honored to have worked collegially and professionally with the following notable military officers all of whom had very successful and distinguished careers in their years of military service for God and Country: LTG Merle Freitag, USA (Ret.), chairman of the MAF committee from 2004-2012; CH (COL) Wayne Lehrer, USA (Ret.) from 2004-2011; CAPT Leroy Vogel, CHC, USN (Ret.), from 2004-2009; Rev. James Behnke, (LTC) USA (Ret.), from 2004-2009; Ch, LtCol Ted Wuerffel USAF (Associate Director 2005-08). RADM James C. Doebler, CEC, USN (Ret.), chairman of the MAF committee from 2012-21; CH (LTC) USA Eric Erkkinen (Assistant Director 2008-14); CH (COL) James Hoke, USA (Ret.), from 2011-2013; CAPT Jonathan Frusti, CHC, USN (Ret.), from 2009-2012; Ch, Lt Col Robert Stroud, USAF (Ret.), from 2009-2015; MAJ Eugene Schneider, USA, (Ret.), from 2013-2022; CH (COL) David Wollenburg, USAF (Ret.), from 2012-2021.

113   Concordia Historical Institute, Footnotes, Vol. 51, Issue 3. https://concordiahistoricalinstitute.org/wp-content/uploads/2014/07/HF51-3.pdf. (accessed May, 2023)

supposed to run for six months turned into a two year display enjoyed by the visiting public.

The turn of the new millennium while promising peace and hope for a brighter world was a time of great stress for America. The average man on the street, in the wake of 9/11 wanted revenge for better or for worse, and the military wanted righteous justice to right the wrongs of 3,000 innocent American civilians murdered. The Iraq war against terrorism commenced March 20th 2003 under the codename of Operation Iraqi Freedom (OIF). The war in Afghanistan codenamed Operation Enduring Freedom (OEF) against terrorism commenced in 2001 until troop withdrawal in 2021 making this war the longest war in US history surpassing even Vietnam by a few months. My entire tenure as endorsing agent was served under the specter of war.

Chaplain Wuerffel (left) and Chaplain Schreiber cut the ribbon for the new Chaplain Corps exhibit at CHI, October 23, 2006.

The US military's new war-footing and build-up meant the mobilization of the nation's Reserve forces which included the call-up of Reserve chaplains from all denominations to active duty in record numbers. Most of our LCMS Reserve chaplains were serving as the sole full-time pastor in their churches. When mobilization orders were issued it meant that their churches would be vacant for the duration of their orders. Initially, many recall orders were 18 months in length. After a couple of years into the war, the orders ranged from 9-12 months on average depending upon the branch of service. Not only did this put great stress upon the chaplain/pastor and his family but also the congregation would suddenly become vacant of its minister. Throughout these war years, many Reserve chaplains were called-up to active duty multiple times.

Together with the MAF committee we worked out the necessary ingredients from the church's perspective for mandatory mobilization agreements to be put in place should the chaplain/pastor be recalled. The MOB agreement guaranteed that the pastor would still be the pastor to his congregation upon return from active duty after his leave of absence. The MOB agreement also created a situational awareness for the congregation and the chaplain/pastor's family to connect them with all military resources available during deployment. MOB agreements are still mandatory for all Reserve chaplains to this day in Synod.

In response to a Synodical convention resolution in 2007, we organized and initiated Operation Barnabas as a distinct ministry in direct support of the Reserve chaplain, his congregation and family. Chaplain Mike Moreno, Captain, US Navy, was called and served as the Project Manager for OB throughout the nation. His excellent work expanded the concept and created a nationwide support system for all our military personnel (veterans, Reserve chaplains and their families) in our congregations. Operation Barnabas is established as a fully operational ministry to this day.

The utilization of tens of thousands of Reservists for the duration of the Iraq and Afghanistan war created a new camaraderie between regular active duty chaplains and reserve chaplains. The vast majority of LCMS Reserve chaplains serving congregations during this time received orders to deploy to a war zone. Many deployed more than once. Upon re-deployment to their home congregations, all Reserve chaplains were invited to attend the MAF annual Professional Training workshop with regular active duty chaplains. Expenses were covered in the same manner as regular active duty chaplains. The inclusion of all Reserve chaplains and their families continues to this day. My years as a chaplain in the Naval Reserve gave me a unique perspective and insight regarding how the church could best utilize and support Reserve chaplains who are pastors of their own congregations with our active duty military force.

In addition, due to the generous increased financial support[114] from our compassionate saints in the pew for our LCMS chaplains through Ministry to the Armed Forces, new initiatives could be envisioned and implemented such as the Doctor of Ministry degree with military concentration. A chaplain endowment fund was established for the degree program held on the campus of Concordia Seminary, St. Louis, that substantially reduced the tuition fees and cost of completing the degree. The DMIN degree was tailored to short intensive two week bursts of academic activity which enabled the chaplain to remain on active duty and still complete the degree program within a 5 year cycle. Many chaplains took advantage of the degree program and added the earned title of Doctor of Ministry to their list of accomplishments and proficiency.

During the Obama administration (2008-2016) when during a lame-duck session of Congress in 2010, DADT[115] was abolished in the military and shortly thereafter DOMA,[116] theologically conservative chaplains across the denominations faced extreme pressure to modify their preaching and counseling ministries against their own consciences to new guidelines that normalized homosexual practices. At that time I was a member of the Executive Committee of NCMAF[117] and raised my voice in concern regarding the chilling effect that dismissal of DADT/DOMA would have upon the free exercise of religion

---

114 Beginning with my second year in office, 2005, MAF received and enjoyed significant surplus budgets every year until 2014.

115 DADT: Don't Ask, Don't Tell was repealed on September 20, 2011 after study and review by the Joint Chiefs of Staff. They concluded that repeal of DADT affecting sexual orientation would not impact military readiness.

116 DOMA: Defense of Marriage Act was signed into law in 1996 under President Bill Clinton banning federal recognition of same-sex marriage. The law was deemed unconstitutional and overturned by Supreme Court decision in the US vs. Windsor case, 2013.

117 NCMAF: National Conference on Ministry to the Armed Forces

THE NEW WORLD OF ENDORSING AGENT

and conscience throughout the military, especially our military chaplains. This led to the creation of the Chaplain Alliance for Religious Liberty[118] which was formed to support and legally defend any and all challenges upon chaplains and their freedom of speech in the engagement of their ministry to military personnel.[119] Chaplain Alliance for Religious Liberty continues to support and defend our military chaplains to this day.

God's script written upon His footprints for my ten years as endorsing agent and Director was a golden script written in celestial ink that I could never have penned or imagined for myself.[120] These major initiatives birthed and established on my watch remain and have borne abundant fruit to this day. They were golden years of ministry.

I would like to pay a special tribute to Chaplain (Lieutenant Colonel) Eric Erkkinen, USA, Retired, who was my Assistant Director for the six years leading up to my retirement, (2008-2014). Eric was a wealth of knowledge on Army military matters, and in addition, Eric had been deployed downrange in 2006 to Baghdad during OIF. Together over many cups of coffee we scrutinized and vetted every chaplain wannabe candidate before presentation to the MAF committee for a vote and endorsement. We initiated, implemented and maintained all ministry programs in support of our chaps. We logged thousands of air miles exercising a robust rotating visitation plan making official visits to all LCMS chaps and their Commands wherever they were stationed

---

118   Chaplain Alliance for Religious Liberty mission statement: *Chaplain Alliance for Religious Liberty* exists to ensure that chaplains can defend and provide for the freedom of religion and conscience that the Constitution guarantees all chaplains and those whom they serve. https://www.chaplainalliance.org/. (accessed April 2, 2023). I served on the original steering committee together with Chaplain Ron Crews and Chaplain Doug Lee in 2011. My successor, Chaplain Craig Muehler, CHC, USN, (Ret.), now Director and Endorsing Agent for The Lutheran Church-Missouri Synod, is the second president to serve Chaplain Alliance.
119   All chaplains from all denominations who provide qualified candidates and endorse such candidates to become military chaplains do so under the understanding that the chaplain will faithfully serve all military personnel without discrimination and at the same time serve in harmony with his/her own church body's confession and doctrinal stance.
120   Ephesians 3:20 Now to Him who is able to do exceedingly abundantly above all that we ask or think, according to the power that works in us, to Him be glory in the church by Christ Jesus to all generations, forever and ever. Amen.

around the world. Eric's penchant for thinking through logical consequences always led me to consider the second and third order of effects for all new ministry approaches conceived and presented for the benefit of the church, our chaplains, their families and their congregations. These were especially good years, years filled with the exciting script of God. All I had to do was to pick up my feet and walk forward. The Lord had promised to keep me in His chosen vocation and bear fruit for His name's sake until the end. He has kept his promise, abundantly.

Chaplain Eric Erkkinen, United States Army. *"My daily coffee buddy."*

Postscriptum

Planning for the golden years of retirement seems like a pleasant task but can be fraught with a few pitfalls all its own. The sudden burst of leisure time upon your daily POD (Plan of the Day) is not only a loss of your former status, prestige and work schedule but a unique recoupling with your spouse, who may or may not enjoy all the time together suddenly available on your marital calendar(!). What is a guy supposed to do? Deploy again?? Well, if he believes in the footsteps of God laid out before him, he will look diligently until he finds it.

I thought I might find it on the golf course in retirement, go on tour, make a million bucks and pay off my house mortgage early but although I'm a pretty fair golfer it is a game that doesn't quite fit my

POSTSCRIPTUM

perfectionist personality. There's always room for improvement in golf which means for me more and more time on the golf course and less and less time exercising the brain for the ministry. Golf became far too addictive to me, time-consuming, expensive and less and less fun. After spending a year on golf "perfecting" my game and multiple rounds clocked at the Grand Haven golf club, my guilty conscience and the Holy Spirit demanded a different routine. I was "nudged" politely by the Almighty and blasted out of the sand trap by His celestial sand wedge.

What to do next? The natural thing, of course, go back to school. Where should I attend? My Alma Mater, of course, Concordia Theological Seminary, Fort Wayne, Indiana. So, back to school I went with my "lunch-box" in hand and my sharpened pencils.

It was wonderful for this ordinary life to walk the halls on the campus from which I graduated in 1977 once again. Hardly anything had changed except for the new multi-million dollar library. What a great place to study! The library was serenely situated contiguous with the large campus pond adjacent to the stunning A-frame chapel. The smell of dusty shelved library books whispered in my ears, "Read me! Read me!" The classroom discussions between the professor and his students stimulated immensely—plus a few cups of coffee—the convoluted contours of my aging brain. And in every class there was one sure-fire guarantee; namely this, I was the oldest "kid" in class and still loving it, probably, one of the oldest students to graduate from the seminary with a PhD at the ancient age of 69, three months shy of my 70th birthday.

I matriculated and attended CTSFW from 2015-2020 completing the PhD missiology degree and "took the walk" the 22nd day of May, 2020.[121] The entire 2019-2020 academic school year was spent

---

[121] The graduation walk was virtual due to COVID, however, the seminary graciously made it up to all graduates by inviting them back on campus for the real thing two years later in May of 2022.

living on campus as a bachelor in the dorms[122] completing the degree program. Monkhood had arrived again. It was another lengthy deployment away from Connie and a thousand miles away from our home in sunny Florida.

My field of study? Moral injury in combat veterans post combat investigating the potential linkage between the high suicide rate and contributing stress factors from combat. The thesis of my doctoral dissertation was the proper reframing of the troubling incident(s)

The newly minted Dr. Schreiber receiving the congratulatory handshake from Dr. Detlev Schulz, the head of the Missiology department, CTSFW.

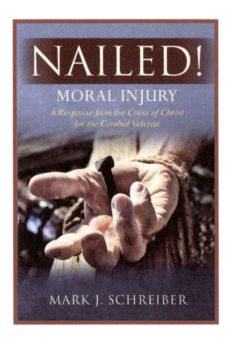

Nailed! Moral Injury: A Response from the Cross of Christ for the Combat Veteran. Published April 2021, Outskirts Press.

---

122 My dorm residence for the academic year was Melanchthon Hall, monk's cell #9.

POSTSCRIPTUM

through the lens of the cross of Christ.[123] The suffering, resurrected Son of God is God's all powerful remedy for moral injury.

Completing the PhD degree had been a long standing dream of mine. It was another footprint of God realized from His divine script. Another leaf had fallen from my earthly tree of life. Extraordinary grace for one ordinary life.

---

123 The interested reader can find my book on moral injury which is distilled from my PhD dissertation at Amazon.com by typing in "Nailed!" and the author's name: Mark J Schreiber, published April, 2021. It is also available at Barnes & Noble and a host of other booksellers.

Epilogue

Baptism is discipleship. If the good works of our Christian life have already been conceived in the mind of God before the foundation of the world (Eph. 2:10) then our entry into this world and especially the date of our baptism marks the beginning of the implementation of God's script for our Christian life. The essence of discipleship is not the literal forsaking of all material goods and then waiting to obey the next voice you hear, rather, the essence of discipleship is to seek out, to discern the will of God according to His Word and to place our feet squarely in His footsteps. The whole baptized Christian life is learning how we ought to walk before God and please Him who first loved us. (1 Thess. 4:1). In fact, St. Paul describes the sanctified life in Christ as a military discipline where the baptized Christian serves as a soldier of Christ focused on pleasing only his Commanding Officer, Christ Jesus, the Lord and Savior of the world. (2 Tim. 2:1-4).

Such discipleship is a strenuous, daily activity maintaining equilibrium between two poles, the negative and positive; the negative, to fight against the Devil, the world and our flesh, and the positive, to seek out the footsteps of God in order to please Him and Him alone. Without the constant grace of your Baptism into Christ Jesus and all that Baptism brings to your life, this task would be impossible.

Furthermore, the footsteps of the Almighty laid out before you will not be discovered passively, as if God would send you a daily email first thing in the morning with the plan of the day attached to it. Wouldn't that be nice? Such a delivery method would leave no room for faith, trust and joy in the unveiling of the exciting script God has already written for your life. If you already knew your future, what need would there be for faith in the promises of God?

Without faith it is impossible to please God. All who seek God's script for their life must first believe in the reality of His presence and that He rewards those who diligently seek Him (Hebrews 11:6). How diligently you seek Him—as urged constantly by the Holy Spirit—is up to you, that is, you have the negative capacity through the presence of the old man to yawn away your entire baptized Christian life, watch TV, drink beer, major in minors, and thus enable the locusts of idleness to devour all the good fruit that could have ripened on the tree of your Christian life. God's script can be avoided and His footsteps can be side-stepped through our own indifference and indolence.

I want a better life for you!

Above the archway written over the main visitor's gate as you enter the spacious courtyard of Luther's house in Wittenberg you will read these words from Dr. Luther *auf Deutsch:*

> *"Niemand lasse den Glauben daran fahren daß Gott an ihm eine große Tat will."*

in other words, in our own mother tongue:

> *Let no one depart from the faith on this point that God wants to work a great work on him.*

Are these words of arrogance from the Reformer as if to say, "How could God not help but do great things through me!" No, Luther's faith flowed from simple trust in the promises of God to guide, to keep and sustain him through the multitude of temptations, vicissitudes, danger and turmoil he faced daily. God's will would be revealed one footstep at a time. Good for Luther. What about you?

The work of God in and through your life is a also a thing of beauty. The evidence surrounds you; it is discernable through the eyes of faith. It is piled high for you just as it is for me. Your ordinary life has been filled with extraordinary grace since the day you were baptized.

Every event in the Savior's life was scripted by God. "The Son of Man indeed goes just as it is written of Him," the Savior said. (Mt. 26:24) And again, "In the scroll of the book it is written of Me. I delight to do your will, O my God," (Ps. 40:7) The Father wanted to do a great work through His Son, and so He did, the greatest work, namely, the salvation of the world. If the greatest story ever told, our Savior's life, has been perfectly scripted by the Father, then how much more will He attend to the details of your life for whom this entire salvation was devoted and delivered?

From cradle to grave, from footsteps of joy to footsteps of sorrow, your ordinary life, one in a billion, baptized into Christ Jesus is a miracle passing through the eye of the needle. Such passage is painful, mandatory and difficult. Without the continual gracious intervening presence of our living God, it would be entirely impossible.

Your life's vignettes have been written by the loving finger of a gracious God. Your last footstep will be your leap across the threshold into Paradise. For you, the Lord Jesus Christ has done it all. Your ordinary life isn't quite as ordinary as you first believed, in fact, it is now quite extraordinary seen and understood through the eyes of faith.

Your heart really wants to know that the living of your life really did make a difference for somebody other than yourself. It wants to know that your whole life was not just a frenzied chase down some narcissistic rabbit hole. Look and believe with an honest heart. Age with the passing of our years wears the spectacles of perspective. The right perspective from the flight deck of God's grace unlocks meaning. Guaranteed.

Only one thing left to do. Let us pray and believe:

POSTSCRIPTUM

Heavenly Father,

Again and again in willful ignorance of your script,

I have boltered across your flight deck of celestial grace.

Again and again you have spun me around and brought me back

to the glide slope of your love, to "call the ball" to land safely

on your divine flight deck.

Grant my heart understanding from your Word

to know and read your script not mine,

to know and comprehend your mission not mine,

that you have scripted for me for your glory.

Get the catapult ready, dear Lord.

Launch my faith heavenward until I see you again,

face to face.

Amen.

Appendix 1

801 DE MUN AVENUE SAINT LOUIS, MISSOURI 63105
TELEPHONE: (314) 721-5934

SCHOOL FOR GRADUATE STUDIES

April 24, 1984

The Rev. Mark Schreiber
68 Longstaff MCAS(H) New River
Jacksonville, NC 28540

Dear Pastor Schreiber:

Your application for admission to the School for Graduate Studies at Concordia Seminary has been reviewed by the faculty Advanced Studies Committee. I am happy to inform you that the action on your application was favorable and that you have been admitted into the STM program in the School for Graduate Studies.

It is our hope that your graduate studies with us will be profitable for both you and the church. We stand ready to assist you in whatever way we can.

Sincerely yours,

Wayne E. Schmidt

Wayne E. Schmidt
Acting Director
Graduate Studies

WES:mln

ENCLOSURE A

A SEMINARY OF THE LUTHERAN CHURCH — MISSOURI SYNOD · FOUNDED 1839

Appendix 2

Rev. Mark J. Schreiber
6519 San Bonita Apt. 2W
Clayton, Mo. 63105

16 January 86
Thursday

Dear Dr. Preus,

    I have reached the end of the road. After careful and prayerful consideration I withdrew from the seminary Friday, January 10th. I have been working as the Coordinator of Reference Services part-time under Dr. Suelflow since September. He has offered me the position on a full-time basis as of 1 February 86. Considering my financial debt, the bleak market in the LCMS school system for STM grads and the potential now to recoup some of my losses, withdrawal seems the most feasible route.

    I have discussed the entire matter with Dr. Klotz, Dean Vogel and Kathy Schlecht (new director of financial aid - Sem. I wife) on more than one occasion with no success. Only Dr. Schmidt (who was the acting director of the graduate school in 84 and knows precisely what I am referring to and urged the committee then to clarify their pocilies when he held the post) and Dr. Suelflow have supported me. Friday morning I and Tom Von Hagel (FW grad, May 85) will speak with Dr. Barth at 11 o'clock. Perhaps some satisfaction can yet be received.

    I recently finished a telephone conversation with Dwight Hellmers who graduated from Springfield in 74 and finished his STM at FW inthe summers. He received the same correspondence I did regarding the Walther fellowship and applied for the same two years in a row (83-84). The first year when he didn't receive the Walther he was offered an application for other graduate study grants. The second year the school sent him the applications for all scholarships _before_ he applied. My correspondence enclosed is very similar. I realized that my chances for the Walther when you wrote my letter of reference were rather slim. I figured the seminary would want a closer look at me. But I felt confident about receiving one of the other substantial graduate study fellowships which I cannot currently apply for, according to Kathy Schlecht, until I become a "St. Louis" grad. This entire graduate school policy is fraudulent and deceptive. The William Scheele foundation is the only source for all graduate fellowships and quarterly grant monies. It is only available to

St. Louis grads according to the policy of the foundation. The foundation has been in existence for twenty years or more and Dr. Klotz knew precisely what their regulations were regarding recpients. Then why is this not clearly stated? Why are other applicants encouraged to apply when in reality they are not even in the competition? I have worked long and hard to maneuver myself into a position financially where I could afford to attend graduate school full-time and support my family. Few, if any other graduate students here are able to do this. Almost all are part-time. I uprooted my family half way across the country, probably left a Navy career in the trashbin, sold all my dining room furniture and my piano of 27 years so we could squeeze ourselves into a two bedroom apartment and for what? Yes, the Lord guides me still. We will survive. But this does not justify the graduate school policy here. To lure a student into a graduate school program with attractive "carrots" only to inform him later that we "just discovered" these carrots are not for your consumption--you're the wrong kind of rabbit--is plainly unconscionable and illegal. . . and this is _my_ Synod.

I could send along my lengthy petition submitted 18 December to the committee regarding a waiver for quarterly grant money but it is not necessary and would be too time consuming for your busy schedule. I do hope that your students are informed of St. Louis's policy. Tom Von Hagel, if he completes his STM here, will pay over $4,000 for the degree out-of-pocket with no $$ at all from the graduate school.

On another matter, I have given serious consideration to your suggestion regarding campus ministry. I have an appointment to see Rev. Ed. Schmidt at 2:15 this Friday (17 January). Enclosed is an outline of my educational resume. I would truly appreciate another good word from you on my behalf to Ed Schmidt. Thank you for your continual support. You, Dr. Suelflow and Dr. Schmidt have been the only lights is this darkness.

May the Lord bless you and yours richly in 86. Say "Hi" to your articulate and gracious wife from the Schreibers!

Trusting in his promises,

Mark

Mark Schreiber

PS. I have also enclosed copies of letters from senior Chaplains advocating my recall to active duty. In some ways what they say clarifies the issue. Blessings.

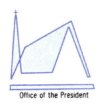

Concordia Theological Seminary

Office of the President

6600 N. Clinton St. / Fort Wayne, Indiana 46825-4996 / (219) 482-9611

January 29, 1986

The Reverend Mark J. Schreiber
6519 San Bonita, Apt. 2W
Clayton, MO 63105

Dear Mark:

I got your January 16 letter with all the materials. I will write a letter to Ed Schmidt recommending you for student work in case you wish to go that direction and in case there is a challenging call available.

In the meantime I plan to follow up and see whether your debaucle is somewhat common. If it is, I am going to get in contact with Dr. Karl Barth and possibly Dr. August Suelflow and tell them that they must change their whole approach to this Walther Fellowship and perhaps others. If you were as mean as some people are in the Missouri Synod, you could probably sue them at the seminary there--not that I am even suggesting such an awful thing! But they are certainly doing something that could be subject to some real litigation, and that ought to be stopped. Meanwhile, you are the victim.

But I have no doubt that the Lord is leading you just as much as when you were on the highest road. Maybe you will get into a situation where you will go to an excellent school and be able to prepare yourself to serve our Synod. In the meantime there are absolutely no places open, I am sure. The colleges are closing down and tightening the belts and so are the seminaries with our lack of enrollment, which next year will be a real disaster. If there is anything more I can do to help you in any way, please don't hesitate to let me know.

Greetings to your dear wife from Donna and me.

Sincerely, in Christ,

Robert Preus

RP:dm

Appendix 3

```
                OFFICE OF THE COMMAND CHAPLAIN
                MARINE CORPS AIR STATION, NEW RIVER
                JACKSONVILLE, NORTH CAROLINA 28545-5000
```

23 December 1985

TO WHOM IT MAY CONCERN

Subj: Mark Schreiber

    This letter is written in support of the Rev. Mark Schreiber in effort to be recalled to active duty in the Chaplain Corps of the United States Navy. I have known the Rev. Schreiber for seven years, first as a Reserve Chaplain and later when he was attached to MAG-29 at MCAS New River. Rev. Schreiber is highly articulate, a superb preacher and administrator, able to get any job assigned accomplished with great skill and efficiency, and one of the outstanding young Chaplains I have known. He is pluralistic in his approach to ministry, and pays meticulous attention to detail while at the same time appearing to do all with ease and grace. Highly educated, obviously spiritual, he relates comfortably and effectively with all to whom he ministers.

    I recommend without hesitation that he be recalled to active duty.

                                    E. H. CAMPBELL, JR.
                                    Captain, Chaplain Corps, U. S. Navy
                                    Command Chaplain

Office of the Command Chaplain
Marine Corps Air Station
New River
Jacksonville, North Carolina 28545-5000

31 January 86

Dear Chaplain Campbell,

I want to sincerely thank you for your outstanding letter of support for my recommendation to recall for active duty. All of the documents needed for my processing are now in the office of Chaplain Goetz. Now, the decision is theirs. Chaplain Shaw (our LCMS endorsing agent) tells me that Chaplain Muchow (LCMS) sits on the board for recall that expects to meet in the May-June timeframe. Chaplain Shaw is optimistic because of that positive connection. Chaplain Goetz, however, is more realistic and neutral. Time will tell.

I cannot thank you enough, Chaplain Campbell, for all your fine support, encouragement and recommendation for at least the chance to be recalled to active duty I do not know if you are an acquaintance of Chaplain Don Muchow but if you happen to run into him at some conference before May any other "good word" would be greatly appreciated.

Thanks again. We will survive. The Lord's richest blessings upon you, Anna Faye and you family in 86. Hope your son Mark is doing much better by now.

Sincerely,

Mark

LT MARK J. SCHREIBER
LT, CHC, USNR

Office of the Wing Chaplain
Second MAW, FMF, Atlantic
Marine Corps Air Station
Cherry Point, North Carolina 28533

31 January 86

Dear Chaplain Weeks,

    I couldn't ask for a finer letter of support for recall to active duty. You are consistent and honest in your support of Chaplains and I appreciate that greatly. All documents that are needed for my processing for recall are now in the office of Chaplain Goetz. Now, only time will tell, the decision is theirs. Chaplain Goetz believes that the board will meet again in the May-June timeframe. Chaplain Don Muchow sits on the board and knows me from Chaplains Basic school in the summer of 1980 and elsewhere. Chaplain Shaw (our LCMS endorsing agent) is optimistic because of that positive connection. However, Chaplain Goetz paints a more neutral and realistic picture.

                                                  Sincerely,

                                                  Mark

                                              LT MARK J. SCHREIBER
                                              LT, CHC, USNR

Messiah Lutheran Church   31 January 86
Chaplain Hugh Lecky
511 North Sellars Mill Road
Burlington, North Carolina 27215

Dear Chaplain Lecky,

    I want to thank you sincerely for your fine letter of support sent out on my behalf in late December to Chaplain Goetz. I couldn't ask for stronger words of recommendation from the Senior Chaplains that I know. All documents and correspondence that needs to be reviewed for my recall is now in Chaplain Goetz's office. The latest word is that the next board meets in the May-June time frame to "pick up the loose ends." Chaplain Don Muchow sits on the same board and Chaplain Shaw (LCMS endorsing agent) say he's optimistic. Chaplain Goetz however, paints a more realistic, neutral picture. Soon, time will tell.

    I thank you again for your support. Blessings up your new adventure in ministry and your family in 86.

                                          Sincerely,

                                          Mark

                                        LT. Mark J. Schreiber
                                        LT, CHC, USNR

Appendix 4

DEC RESNAVADMIN FY-04

R 241621Z NOV 03 ZYB MIN PSN 475860J30

FM CNO WASHINGTON DC//N1//

TO NAVADMIN

UNCLAS //N01421//
NAVADMIN 303/03

MSGID/GENADMIN/CNO WASHINGTON DC/N1/-/NOV//

SUBJ/NAVAL RESERVE PROMOTIONS TO THE GRADES OF CAPTAIN,
/COMMANDER, LIEUTENANT COMMANDER, LIEUTENANT, LINE
/AND STAFF CORPS, AND WARRANT OFFICERS//

RMKS/1. CONGRATULATIONS TO THE FOLLOWING OFFICERS ON THEIR
PROMOTIONS TO THE RANKS INDICATED IN THIS MESSAGE. THIS NAVADMIN
IS THE AUTHORITY FOR EFFECTING TEMPORARY AND PERMANENT OFFICER
PROMOTIONS WHICH ARE EFFECTIVE ON THE DATES INDICATED.
READ NAME, LAST FOUR DIGIT SSN/DESIG
CAPTAIN LINE AND STAFF SENATE CONFIRMATION DATE
LINE 27 JUNE 2003   STAFF 27 JUNE 2003
DOR/EFF   1 OCTOBER 2002
OTTLINGER MICHAEL ERNE 6363/1105   STONE ROBERT E   3383/1635
DOR/EFF   1 DECEMBER 2003
ADAMS GREGORY SCOTT   4652/1635   AFONG DANFORD SCOTT KA 2660/1115
ALLEN HARRY WILLIAM   0182/1635   AUSTIN CLAYTON BARTHOL 9747/1115
BOONE DERRICK SHERROD 4304/1115   BUDI PETER NMN   9471/3105
BUXTON ROBERT D   6159/1117   CASH CHARLES EDWIN   1364/1315
COCHRANE JOHN CAMPBELL 7012/1115   DOMERACKI HENRY STEFAN 0831/1635
ERNST KEVIN MICHAEL   8142/1115   FENSKE DOUGLAS WILLIAM 0137/1637
FINK DANIEL CHARLES   2591/1315   GERBINO PETER G II   6072/2105
GIDEON JEFFREY LUKE   4871/1315   GILMAN NANCY HOOSER   5715/2905
GORDON LANCE BENNETT   3804/1635   GRENFELL NORMA JEANNE 7911/2905
GUREKIAN PATTI R   0569/1105   HAZARD SHERRILL JOHN I 3281/1115
HOOVER RONALD LEE   4237/1635   HOYT ROGER BRETT   0917/1115
HUGHES STEPHEN DWIGHT 1928/3105   JACKMORE JAMES ANTHONY 7709/1635
KAISER CLIFFORD YALMER 7110/1125   KELLER RAYMOND JR   3458/1635
LANCE LEEROY JR   9249/1635   LOVEJOY DENNIS LLOYD   2057/1635
LUCAS PATRICIA ANN   2399/1635   MAREADY DAVID WILLIAM 0566/1635
MCCARTHY LYNN ANN   6676/1107   NETH SAMUEL LEONARD   7843/1115
NEY MARK DAVID   4898/1635   POWELL LEE ANNE BRIGHT 9145/2905
ROBERTS CHARLES TERRY 4722/1635   SCHLESINGER LINDA JOAN 0682/3105
SCHREIBER MARK JAMES   7579/4105   THOMAS JESSE DANIEL   8077/3105
VOLKOFF JOHN   2260/1635   WALSTON DAVID EDWARD   4847/2305
WHEATLEY RICHARD TUDOR 7567/1315   WITHERS PETER ALEX   3045/1635
WOLFE RICHARD EARLE   3818/2305

Appendix 5

Printed in the USA
CPSIA information can be obtained
at www.ICGtesting.com
JSHW071045071123
51469JS00025B/168